Texas Edible Wild Plant Foraging

Beginner Foraging Field Guide for Finding, Identifying, Harvesting, and Preparing Edible Wild Food

By
Willow Walsh

© Copyright Willow Walsh 2022 - All rights reserved.

The content contained within this book may not be reproduced, duplicated or transmitted without direct written permission from the author or the publisher.

Under no circumstances will any blame or legal responsibility be held against the publisher, or author, for any damages, reparation, or monetary loss due to the information contained within this book. Either directly or indirectly. You are responsible for your own choices, actions, and results.

Legal Notice:

This book is copyright protected. This book is only for personal use. You cannot amend, distribute, sell, use, quote or paraphrase any part, or the content within this book, without the consent of the author or publisher.

Disclaimer Notice:

Please note the information contained within this document is for educational and entertainment purposes only. All effort has been executed to present accurate, up to date, and reliable, complete information. No warranties of any kind are declared or implied. Readers acknowledge that the author is not engaging in the rendering of legal, financial, medical or professional advice. The content within this book has been derived from various sources. Please consult a licensed professional before attempting any techniques outlined in this book.

By reading this document, the reader agrees that under no circumstances is the author responsible for any losses, direct or indirect, which are incurred as a result of the use of the information contained within this document, including, but not limited to, — errors, omissions, or inaccuracies.

TABLE OF CONTENTS

Introduction I

PART – I: A Beginner's Guide To Foraging 6

Chapter 1: What Is This New Trend? 7
    The Benefits of Foraging 10

Chapter 2: The Matters of Sustainability 12
    Is Foraging the Sustainable Food System We Can Turn to? 14

Chapter 2: A: Ethical Foraging – A Sound and Sustainable Way .. 18
    What is Ethical Foraging? 18
    Principles of Ethical Foraging 21

Chapter 2-B: The Impact of Foraging on Wild Plants 24
    Native Plant Species 24
    Non-native Plant Species 25
    The Impact of Foraging on Plants 28

Chapter 3: Nature's Gift – Wild Edible Plants 30
    What are Wild Edible Plants? 30
    Major Groupings of Wild Edible Plants 33

Chapter 4: Parts of a Plant – An Identification Guide 35
    Identification Methods 37
    The Methodology for Identifying Plants 39
    On-the-go Resources 41

Chapter 5: The Matters of Safety 42

    The Universal Edibility Test 43

    Identify Poisonous Plants 45

    Tools and Safety Equipment 46

PART – II: Foraging In Texas 48

Chapter 6: Laws of the Land 49

    Foraging Rules in Texas 49

    Foraging Do's and Don'ts in Texas 51

Chapter 7: Where to Forage in Texas? 54

    Rural foraging in Texas 54

    Urban foraging in Texas 57

    Where not to forage in Texas 59

    Rules for foraging 60

Chapter 8: What to Forage in Texas? 61

    FAQs About Wild Edible Plants Found in Texas 61

Chapter 9: How to Harvest Edible Plants 67

    Harvesting Leaves and Greens 68

    Harvesting Greens 69

    Harvesting Leaf Shoot / Leaf Stalk "Spears" 69

    Harvesting Stems 69

    Harvesting The Whole Plant 70

    Harvesting Barks 70

    Harvesting Flowers 70

    Harvesting Flower Buds 71

    Harvesting Seeds and Nuts 71

    Harvesting Roots 72

    Harvesting Fruit 72

    Harvesting Cacti 72

Chapter 10: Storage and Preservation 101 74

    Standard Storage Practices 74

    Preserving Foraged Wild Plants 76

PART – III: Texas Wild Edible Plant Almanac 82

Directory 1: Plant Profiles and Seasonal Charts 83

    Plant Profiles 84

    Seasonal Chart 166

    Poisonous Plants 169

Directory 2: 10 Recipes from Wild Plants 180

Conclusion 188

References 195

A FREE GIFT TO OUR READERS

20 EDIBLE WILD PLANT RECIPES

www.willowwalsh.com

FREE GIFT TO OUR READER

FORAGING JOURNAL PDF DOWNLOAD

INTRODUCTION

"Earth was not built for six billion people all running around and being passionate about things. The world was built for about two million people foraging for roots and grubs." - Douglas Coupland, Canadian Novelist

Before factories, before commercial farms, before grocery stores, before we could press a button and have breakfast, lunch, and dinner brought straight to our doorsteps, humans survived from day-to-day in one way: Foraging – using the plants and animals provided by nature as food.

Slowly, the activity was pushed back to give way to more modern ways of gaining the sustenance we need to nourish our bodies. In recent times, however, foraging has been brought back into the spotlight. People are marveling at the health benefits and its psychological advantages, too. It is all the fad now, gaining attention in different types of media.

But foraging is not a new phenomenon. It is not a fad that will fade into a fond memory like the era of bell-bottom pants. It is a practice that has existed as part of human culture throughout our history.

In fact, more than 90% of the time that human beings have been evolving on this planet has been sustained by foraging. We are by nature, foragers, adapted to hunt for and gather our food. After all, 200,000 years of evolution have ingrained the activity into our DNA. Even before the first modern-day humans appeared, our Homo sapien ancestors foraged for millions of years.

Even though the economics of commercializing food sources has taken us away from our roots of foraging, there are still many communities on this planet that still rely on such a way of life, and show that it is very much a viable way of getting the food that we need to survive. The Bushmen of Southern Africa are an example of foragers surviving and thriving in modern-day society. Their people have been living in the semi-desert areas of South Africa, Namibia, and Botswana for more than 30,000 years. The arid condition of those areas can make life difficult, yet these people are not only innovatively finding ways to gain their water supply needs but also feeding themselves both in the dry and wet seasons with edible wild plant life. They do this with primitive tools like cloaks to carry their finds and digging sticks to locate the nature-given goodies which include fruits, berries, and young shoots.

Foraging has been a big part of human history – and it exposed our ancestors to a variety of foods that provided for our nutritional needs. We live in a time where everything moves in the fast lane and that includes the way we eat. Fast food, drive-thrus, processed foods...we are living on a diet meant to suit such a pace, but is this way of eating really benefiting us? The alarming rising cases of obesity and diet-related illnesses and diseases like diabetes and heart disease are consequences we can't ignore. The decreased quality of life and even premature death have become a reality because of how we eat. This is forcing us to take a step back and reevaluate how we nourish ourselves and what we eat. It has made us take a look at the past where cultures of people lived off the land

and benefited nutritionally. The Bushmen of Africa are not the only modern examples of people still foraging and experiencing the benefits. Deep in the Amazon, the ancient Tsimane Indian tribes, the Arctic Inuit, Hadza... in all different locations around the planet and all sorts of environments, from hot to cold, from desert to forest, people are using what many would deem a Stone Age diet and they are thriving physically. With all the trendy diets that come and go, foraging seems to be the only true diet that fits the genetic makeup of humans and so our bodies take to it naturally.

Even though modern Homo sapiens appeared around 200,000 years ago, farming for sustenance has not been around as long. In fact, the agricultural practice is dated somewhere between 12,000 and 23,000 years old. Farms popped up across the globe for different reasons and at different times. China started harvesting rice. Western Asia started harvesting wheat. West Africa planted yams, corn was harvested in Central America, and potatoes were in the Andes. However, before then, we humans survived hundreds of thousands of years exclusively by hunting animals and gathering wild plants. While farming can offer a steady food supply barring extreme conditions like drought and flooding, it also has many disadvantages associated with it. It led to a population boom, but it also led to:

- Warring over land
- The use of slave labor to keep these farms
- Widespread famine when sudden extreme conditions meant failed crops
- Environmental degradation
- Infringement of animal rights and diseases due to close

proximity to animals

Regarding eating practices specifically, farming limits the amount and variety of foods that we consume. Foraging for wild plants means that anything edible can go into your tummy. Eating is limited to the crops that have been planted when farming. For example, rice is a staple meal item in China because the crop is planted heavily there. The same is true for yams in West Africa and corn in Central America. This lack of variety means less nutrition is available to us. History proves this. Archaeological digs discovered the teeth and bones of foragers and study of them shows that they were less disease-ridden compared to their counterparts who relied on farming to eat. We now live in an agricultural-based society and while we have made many advances technologically, we can reflect on the practices of our foraging ancestors and learn a lot. In some ways, we have started seeing the shift in mindset as more and more people are acknowledging the advantages of living off the land rather than relying on agriculture. The rising popularity of eating practices that mimic times before farming became the norm is one such example. With such diets, foods that are farmed like grains and legumes are limited and emphasis is placed on foods that can be hunted and gathered.

Individually, we can make strides in that regard because foraging opens up doors of limitless possibilities from a nutritional standpoint. You can fulfill your nutritional needs in their entirety with a vast array of foods that you can put your own spin on with tasty recipes. You don't have to compromise on flavor.

Food prices are skyrocketing in the face of global plights like wars and pandemics. The quality of foods on grocery shelves has continued to decrease, having been created from questionable standards. Nutrition is compromised with artificial ingredients and high levels of food processing. We are killing ourselves with a

practice - feeding ourselves - meant to ensure longevity. We need a better way of eating. Luckily, we don't have to reinvent the wheel. The answer to our problem has existed for hundreds of thousands of years. Foraging is our opportunity to gain better nutrition as well as a way to get closer to nature and connect through the environment. Whether you are tired of spending too much on expensive supermarket food that is machine-processed to wash away the nutritional value or dislike buying food that is grown under questionable circumstances, foraging is the solution that solves your plight. It is a source of natural food that is available anywhere if you know how to look. You can do it at any time and it has virtually zero cost. Say goodbye to long exorbitant grocery bills. This book was written to show you how and what to forage in Texas specifically. You will learn:

- How to identify the edible parts of 40 different wild plants growing across the state
- How to forage ethically and sustainably
- How to forage in Texas with an emphasis on the habitats to explore and how to be well-prepared for safe foraging
- The risks associated with poisonous plants and how to avoid them
- Recipes for transforming wild plants into tasty cuisine for any occasion
- And more!

Let's hop right into this adventure featuring foraging in Texas. Turn the page to read more.

PART – I
A Beginner's Guide To Foraging

CHAPTER 1

WHAT IS THIS NEW TREND?

Before you can take on any new task or activity, you first need to understand what it is you are doing. The same goes for foraging. Therefore, the first thing we must take on is defining what foraging is and what foragers do. Foraging is an experience. So many times, the act of eating gets lost in all the things we do on a daily basis as a mindless to-do. We do it only to survive because we would perish otherwise. We stuff food into our mouths, chew, swallow and move on to the next thing. But if we would only take the time to slow down and consciously and deliberately eat, the experience could be something magical rather than mundane. Foraging allows you to make eating magical. To forage, you must wander and look around you to see things that could have otherwise passed under your radar. You need to look around you with new eyes. Foraging makes eating an adventure. You not only explore to find the wild foods that suit your palate, but you also appreciate the fruits of your labor more and thus, put more effort into savoring them when they do eventually reach your mouth. While some people might simply call foraging the "act of finding and harvesting wild food," I call it a delicate art form that transforms gathering food that grows without interference by humans into a mindful practice that allows for appreciating what we put into our bodies. And that is what foragers do - use what nature provides with a mindset of appreciation.

As a more scientific layout of what foraging is, it entails the locating, identification, and collection of wild food. Foraging is an absolutely normal part of our everyday lives. Think about it. Any time that you have gone camping or have been in a park and you located a fruit and ate it, you have foraged. As children, we loved to indulge in fruit that we found in our backyards or at school, or while walking along the road. All of these are examples of foraging. Any wild plant that has been picked and eaten from an uncultivated area has been an item that has been foraged.

Wild food is the center of what makes foraging the activity that it is. So, this book would not be complete without an outline of what exactly wild food is. Wild food is any plant that grows without human management and has been gathered for consumption. Fish and game are examples of wild foods. Plants that grow without cultivation are also examples of wild foods and are called wild plants. The parts of wild plants that can be edible include their fruit, flowers, flower buds, stems, leaves... in fact, an entire plant can be edible. The trick is to understand exactly which parts of the plant are edible and not poisonous to you before you indulge.

Foragers are the ones who gather these wild foods for indulgence. Being a forager means that you have to be resourceful as you have to explore and familiarize yourself with the area that you forage in as well as the seasons that plants are plentiful in and can be harvested. You respect the land and the habitats that wild foods grow in. Anyone, from any background and of any age, can become a forager. It is a skill that simply takes time and patience in which to develop competence. A good place to start honing these skills is reading good foraging books such as this one. Get as much "book

smarts" as you can about wild plants and then venture into your local parks and uncultivated public areas and apply what you have learned. You need to learn the landscape and common plants that grow there. Pay attention to the small details like the shape of leaves, the color of flowers, the average height of that plant species, and how these things change from season to season. Be sure that you are able to confidently identify plants before you decide to eat them.

Apart from your local parks and public uncultivated spots, common places to forage include:

- Woodland areas
- Open fields
- Coastlines
- Forests
- Footpaths
- Hedgerows

Even your backyard can serve as an uncultivated spot for foraging. Anywhere can serve as a foraging area as long as there are wild plants to be harvested. A note of caution, though. Get permission from the owners or management of the property before you forage on private land. Also, nature reserves have specific rules for foraging, so be sure to familiarize yourself with them before using such land for that activity.

Summer, fall, and spring are typically highly fruitful when it comes to foraging. However, winter is not to be completely discarded. While there are a few options typically, if you know how and where to look, you can rustle up some tasty wild plants. There is no time of year when you cannot feel like a foraging champion when you gather the wild plants that can provide all your nutritional needs.

THE BENEFITS OF FORAGING

For some time, foraging has been seen as a rustic and primitive activity by many, but interest has been rising over the last few years. This interest has only increased during the 2020 pandemic when more people were forced to stop and take notice of what was going on around them and connect with nature. As a result, the benefits of foraging have been placed in the spotlight. That reconnection with nature is one such benefit. Far too many of us have been chained to desks and confined to concrete jungles. We all need the opportunity to unplug from our daily life and reduce our stress levels. Foraging gives you the opportunity to get off the beaten path and stop to smell the roses, all while getting in exercise and seeing new, interesting nature elements that are not limited to just plant life. You become more mindful and appreciative of all nature has to offer.

Apart from being good for your pocket and giving you the nutrition you need, other benefits of foraging include:

- It can be done anywhere and in any environment including urban spaces
- Foraging introduces something new to your palate and is a great way for discovering new flavors
- It is a great way to help you experiment with food
- Foraging allows you to take up a new hobby
- It allows you to continuously learn new things
- Foraged foods can be fermented and used to make wines and spirits
- Foraging helps you reduce your carbon footprint and is a great way to show that you care about the environment
- Foraged foods are 100% fresh and organic

Now you know what foraging is and how it is beneficial for not only you, but also the people around you on this planet. But, what about the environment? Can an activity that takes away from the

environment also be beneficial for it? Let's discuss this frankly in the next chapter.

CHAPTER 2

THE MATTERS OF SUSTAINABILITY

You might be thinking: *My food demands are still met by modern agriculture in a lot of ways. So, why is foraging a necessary skill to learn?*

While it might be true that modern agriculture caters to your current needs, what about the future? And what about other parts of the world that are struggling to have their food needs met? Modern agriculture might appear to be able to feed everyone all over the world, but it is not sustainable. At least, not in the be-all-end-all sense. M. S. Swaminathan, the father of India's Green Revolution, said it best: "If agriculture fails, everything else will fail."

The human population has surged to 8 billion people in what seems an evolutionary blink of an eye. This growing population is largely in part to the practice of contemporary agriculture. We have developed the systems put in place by our homo sapien forefathers using science and machinery to replace manual labor. As a result of this (along with developments in healthcare like vaccines and antibiotics), the human population has tripled since the mid-20th century. There is no denying the advances that modern agriculture has allowed us. However, using agriculture to sustain such a large population has led to overexploitation of our land and other natural resources:

- Loss of soil.
- Chemical pollution.
- Death of ecosystems.
- Climate change.
- Pollution of water supplies.
- Degrading quality of water...

There is no denying the detrimental impact on our planet, and this strain will only grow as our population continues to grow. Modern agriculture is unsustainable. It already occupies more than 35% of our terrestrial land surface.

Don't get me wrong; it is not that agriculture itself has no future for us. What I mean to say is that if we continue at this pace, we increase the planet's vulnerability to global disasters, which spells doom for us. Humanity's food demands are growing, and we need other ways to supplement and override our dependence on agriculture to feed ourselves. This train of thought was supported by the conclusion reached when food science from around the globe convened in Sydney in 2016:

> *Access to diverse nutritious food and potable water is a right for all life. Our current food systems supporting humans, domestic animals and plants are neither sustainable nor ecologically sound. An integrated and holistic approach involving the whole of society is needed to reverse unsustainable trends within current food systems. (https://modernfarmer.com/2019/10/is-agriculture-sustainable/)*

This is not a one-off warning that we need an alternative way of feeding our growing population. A report from the EAT-Lancet

Commission in early 2019 stated that:

> *Food systems have the potential to nurture human health and support environmental sustainability; however, they are currently threatening both.*

The failings of our agriculture system are impossible to deny. It is simply unsustainable and turning a blind eye to this will only lead to severe consequences in the not-too-distant future.

IS FORAGING THE SUSTAINABLE FOOD SYSTEM WE CAN TURN TO?

With the signs that we are using up our natural resources at too quick of a rate for them to replenish themselves, sustainability has become a hot topic. We, as a species, need to survive. We need to eat to live. With a population that is approaching 10 billion, and assuming the average person eats between 1,500 and 2,000 pounds of food per year, it is understandable that we are running through our resources quickly. But is there a way to give ourselves the things we need without destroying the planet? The answer to that question boils down to sustainability.

We do not have to be an evil to the environment to survive. For far too long we have compartmentalized ourselves away from our natural world: the world where flora, fauna, events, and processes exist without the interference of or interjection from people. We develop cities and urban centers and continually remove ourselves away from what is considered wild. This leads to the idea of preservation vs. conservation.

Preservation holds true to the idea that human beings should not interfere with what is natural. There should be no trace of us there. The forests, the sky, the seas... all of it should remain apart from us and us apart from them. That can hardly be the case when we need

to take from nature to survive. Preservation is often a losing battle because of our dependence on nature and all she gives. As a result, we beat ourselves into the ground when we inevitably cross those lines that we marked for ourselves.

On the other hand, conservation means interacting with nature so that we can take from it in a way that ensures that future generations continue to receive fruits from that land. This is where the sustainability factor comes to life. Foraging is an act of conversation that allows us to interact with and take from nature.

The question still remains - is foraging indeed sustainable? Is it just as harmful as modern agriculture? Does it harm habitats or destroy wildlife? Let's explore this now.

To be clear, any action that we perform that involves taking from nature has the potential to be unsustainable due to how it is accomplished. If we pick and pick from nature as we forage without allowing the wild plants ample time to regrow or trample in the environments in which these plants grow carelessly, then yes, these actions will destroy the wildlife.

This can become a problem when we forage for commercial gains. That is, we forage to sell. In such a case, wild plants can be harvested on a level that does not allow the plants in that space to replenish themselves at a level that keeps up with the demand for that wild plant. Still, commercial foraging does not have to become a menacing activity. It can be controlled so that it is done mindfully and with full transparency so that consumers understand the repercussions of using that land and its resources. This means adhering to local harvesting laws, not using chemicals to change the land, and keeping harvesting activities to specific spaces such as privately owned land.

Foraging is more frequently done on an individual level, though. This is called hobby foraging and it is the focus of this book. This

type of foraging is meant to sustain eating needs on a much smaller level such as ensuring one gets dinner. If you pick a handful of berries while taking a leisurely walk or pick a few shoots to add to your dinner plate, this is hobby foraging. This activity can also become unsustainable if you recklessly trample on the flora and disturb wildlife while you pass through the unbeaten path, or you take more than you need only to waste your pickings. Then hobby foraging bridges into the territory of being unsustainable. Also, as more and more people catch on to this trending train of foraging, certain areas may become over-foraged.

You will notice a common thread here: foraging is only as sustainable as how we go about doing it. Be mindful and ethical whether commercial foraging or hobby foraging, and the wild plant life will continue to thrive even as we take from the land. Remember these rules for sustainable foraging:

1. Be careful to not destroy any flora or fauna life while you forage
2. Leave the land as unchanged as possible while foraging
3. Only take what you need
4. Preserve any leftovers to use later
5. Follow the local harvesting laws to avoid over-foraging

Following these rules allows foraging to be good for the environment since we can aid more plants to grow by dispersing seeds over a wider area and even aiding in pollination. We can help the growth of plants through pruning and small acts like moving branches enough so that sunlight streams in to allow smaller shoots to get the needed rays for photosynthesis. In these small ways, it's been proven that foraging (when done with a mindset for sustainability and continuity) can increase the biodiversity of a habitat.

Texas Edible Wild Plant Foraging

(https://www.researchgate.net/publication/337497053_Urban_Foraging_Its_Role_in_Conservation_and_Green_Space_Management_in_London)

CHAPTER 2

A: ETHICAL FORAGING – A SOUND AND SUSTAINABLE WAY

The key takeaway from the previous chapter is that foraging is only as sustainable as how ethically it is done. But what does it mean to be an ethical forager? This chapter explores the concept and outlines how you can take from the land without scarring it.

WHAT IS ETHICAL FORAGING?

Ethical foraging is the act of developing a symbiotic relationship with the land and the plant life that it produces. This means there is reciprocity between you and the land. You respect it and what it gives to us. You do not just pick and take from it without thought or care. For that to happen, there is a particular mindset that you need to develop long before you ever start foraging.

Most often, any act of unsustainability that we perpetrate against the things that nature gives to us occurs because of a lack of awareness. We do not understand the impact of our actions. Sometimes we are willingly blind to the ramifications because of temporary advantages, but once we take the time to slow down and just look at all that has been done to nature and the consequences this has for humanity, we can change the way we do things. Overforaging has occured in many places largely due to the high demand for a particular plant item. But when you start respecting nature and not indiscriminately taking from it, you start to consider how even the smallest action affects nature's processes.

Ways that you can develop your awareness include:

- Learning about the plants that are most at risk for being overforaged in the area in which you forage. Forage those that are low risk and avoid or limit your use of those that are higher risk.

- Looking into the local laws for the area that you forage. Not only should you ensure that you are not trespassing onto private property, but it is also a great idea to check with the local Forest Service, Parks & Recreations, as well as Fish & Wildlife services to get a feel for the right way to go about foraging in parks, wooded areas, and forests. You can even talk with skilled and experienced local farmers and hunters as they are typically knowledgeable about such things. Gaining this information also helps you avoid fines and legal penalties.

- Learn to identify plants. Not only can this save your life by preventing poisoning, but it can also save plant life by ensuring you do not waste wild plants by picking the wrong plant or its parts for use. Characteristics that you can use to identify plants include their fruits; leaf sizes, types, and edges; flowers; stems; smells; locations; life cycles; and the soil conditions that the plant is growing in. We will go more into identification techniques later in this book. Ways that you can increase your knowledge of such characteristics include going for plant identification walks and using field guides to study.

- Use the right tools and attire to forage. How you harvest a plant is also a point that determines how ethical the act is. If you are twisting and jerking at a plant to get its leaves, flowers, or fruit, you are harming that plant and making it more difficult to reproduce more of that item. I remember once seeing someone shake a tree so that its fruit fell to the ground. He proceeded to only pick up a few of them and walked away. Such a waste! However, the right tools and gear allow you to neatly harvest the parts that you need without harming the plant any more than necessary.

Being an ethical forager is not a one-and-done practice. It is a commitment to a particular code of conduct. You are showing that you care for not only the environment but also yourself and the rest of humanity--even future generations to come. If we in the present day do not protect nature, then there will be nothing for our children and their children to gain from the abundance that we can testify that there is today. When you forage, be sure to:

- Leave the area as good as or even better than you first found it. Disturb the space as little as possible.

- Harvest from safe areas. Avoid areas like busy roadsides, property lines, and industrial areas as these lands tend to have pollutants. Also, scope out the territory that you plan to forage ahead of time so that you can be sure it is safe and that you walk in with the right tools and clothing to protect yourself and the wild plants.

- Only harvest the items you need. Never take more than necessary. As a rule of thumb, never take more than ⅓ of the wild food item that you come across. So, if a plant has 30 fruits, do not pick more than 10 of them. Ideally, you should take even less than this, especially if that plant part is at risk of being over-harvested. You can be more liberal with lower-risk plants. Also, be sure to replace plant items that you are able to such as seeds to ensure future growth.

PRINCIPLES OF ETHICAL FORAGING

It touches my heart to know that people are increasingly seeing the benefits and advantages of foraging. However, the issue of sustainable foraging is a huge one as I would hate to see foraging turn into a practice that harms nature rather than aids it or us. Lack of education and the absence of mindfulness can lead to overzealous behavior when it comes to taking from what nature provides. You can do your part to protect nature while also reaping from its spoils. You can do this by:

- Knowing your environment. Do not allow ignorance to be the reason why you contribute to unsustainable foraging. Pick up field guides about your area from bookstores and local libraries. Learn to identify the characteristics of the plants that are safe to forage in your area. Talk to professional foragers. There are plenty of resources that you can use to become familiar with the regions that you plan to forage and the plant life that grows there. Be innovative and seek knowledge always.

- Develop a foraging plan. Before you step foot out of your door, ensure that you know what you are looking for and exactly where you are going. This needs to be done for several reasons that include keeping yourself safe by planning for potential dangers as well as keeping true to the motto of only picking what you need when harvesting wild plants.

- Always confirm the identity of the plants that you plan to harvest. Do not rely on identifying plants by only one characteristic. Be sure to positively make three points of identification before harvesting the plant. This will ensure as little waste as possible and help prevent poisoning.
- Never harvest wild plants from polluted areas. Ensure that any wild plants that you pick are safe for consumption.

In my time as a forager, I have learned to apply three basic principles that keep my foraging activities safe, ethical, and sustainable:

1. Forage mindfully

Harvest in a way that is sustainable for generations even hundreds of years from now. Always come to the unbeaten path with an air of gratitude and respect. ***Take only what you need.*** I cannot emphasize this enough. There is no need to harvest an entire plant if you only need a few leaves or fruits. Learn ways to preserve what you do take so that it lasts as long as possible and waste is limited. Remember that the long-term survival of wild plants means the long-term survival of the human species.

2. Take care of nature and it will take care of you

Give back to nature in the same way that it gives to us. Whatever we give, it will reciprocate 10 times over. Ways that you can do this include cultivating and spreading wild plants. Simple ways of doing this include scattering seeds and dividing and replanting roots. Particularly target these efforts at high-risk plants so that their populations can become more stabilized. Be sure that as much as you take from nature, you are giving back.

3. Continuously learn

It needs to be an ethical forager's quest to understand the plants that are being harvested and that means more than their identifying characteristics. You need to know these plants' place in the

ecosystem that they grow in and how their population affects that area. One of the best ways to build that knowledge base is to observe and interact safely with plants. Also, build your book smarts, attend workshops, and use your library resources. There is no shortage of ways that you can absorb this knowledge into your noggin. One of my favorite ways for doing so is to connect with like-minded individuals. In this day and age, you are not limited to only offline methods but rather you can connect, learn, and share with online communities.

We have talked about how we can sustainably forage. But what really is the impact of foraging on plants — native, non-native, as well as invasive? We will discuss this in the coming chapter.

CHAPTER 2-B:

THE IMPACT OF FORAGING ON WILD PLANTS

There are three types of plants that can be foraged in any one region. They are native, non-native, and invasive species. The ethics of foraging practice expands to include all of them, which we will discuss in this chapter.

NATIVE PLANT SPECIES

Native plants occur naturally in an environment without being introduced there by human intervention. Such plants help support the balance in that habitat because they have adapted over hundreds or thousands of years to that space. Unfortunately, increases in human population and so, demand increases have led to many of these native plant species being overharvested.

Also called overexploitation, overharvesting is the act of acquiring wild plants (and other natural resources to the point that the practice becomes unsustainable and there is a threat of no longer benefiting from that resource. Overharvesting is one of the five main reasons that plant life is killed off from their natural habitats. The other reasons are habitat fragmentation (the process of a large expanse of habitat being broken down into smaller, displaced spaces), habitat destruction, pollution, and the introduction of invasive plant species.

Overharvesting threatens to make these plant species go extinct and so, this is a threat to the biodiversity of that habitat. It can lower the quality of the plant resources found in the area as well. For example, if bigger leaves were harvested from a particular plant before, smaller leaves may have to be harvested because the plant is no longer growing as big as it used to due to being harvested too much and too often. There are direction negative consequences to humans, as well. If we use many native plants to make medicines and these were to disappear or become limited in supply, we risk suffering from the illnesses they help control.

It is important that we protect the native species that we forage to maintain the balance of that habitat. To do that, we must adhere to the local laws that protect them.

NON-NATIVE PLANT SPECIES

Also called exotic plants, non-native plants are species that do not occur naturally in a habitat. They were introduced by human beings, typically from foreign countries. Often this occurs because of cultivation practices. On the other hand, when a non-native plant grows quickly and its growth threatens the plant community of that habitat, it is known as an invasive species. But what makes it so that a plant species is called invasive? Let's look at that now.

Technology has made it so that the globalization of people is our culture as a species. But this international travel is not just limited to human beings. Plants are not remaining rooted in one spot anymore. They are also wandering the globe and away from their native homes. Often, plants that are not native to an environment die quickly because the conditions are not right for their growth. On the other extreme end of things, there are non-native plants that thrive in this new environment, so much so that they reproduce quickly and threaten to overtake the habitat of native plants. These are called invasive plant species, and their presence can cause negative environmental, health, and economic consequences. The introduction of new plants to different locations can be intentional, but the ill consequences of doing so may not have been realized beforehand. Other times, new species of plants were brought in to control the population of other invasive species but that attempt only led to the introduction of another invasive species. Sometimes, the introduction of an invasive species is not intentional. It can occur accidentally through means like shipping or human travel. It can also be carried by natural forces like wind and sea and ocean currents to new locations.

Most often, the reason that these plants thrive in a foreign environment is that they do not have natural predators in that space. Prey and predator relationships are complex and typically develop naturally over years of evolution. However, when a new plant enters a location, predators often do not have the evolutionary traits that would allow them to exploit that plant's weakness. For example, insects in that area may not have the adaptive anti-venom for the venom that this plant produces to ward off predatory feeders. As a result, the plant does not get eaten or used like other plants in that area where their weaknesses are indeed exploited by the insects that have adapted to their characteristics.

Another reason why non-native plants may be deemed invasive is that they are able to use resources in this location that native plants are not able to. This particular phenomenon is called ecological facilitation.

Texas Edible Wild Plant Foraging

The negative consequences of the presence of invasive plant species include:

- The loss of the natural habitat as the invasive species kills off the native plant species.
- The destruction of the natural habitat because of the plant's use of the resources at a faster than sustainable rate.
- An impact on human health as they may release toxins and other poisonous chemicals in the environment that can pollute other plant life, the soil, and water sources nearby.
- Economic mayhem to control their growth and to clean up the other consequences of their presence.

Apart from obeying the laws to not introduce new plant species to any environment, you can help minimize their negative effects by giving them the spotlight during your foraging trips. That is, you can harvest more than the recommended limits of these plants to help control their spread through the habitat. What you need to remember is to ensure that identification is made before you harvest the plant. Some of these plants have lookalikes that are non-invasive and benefit that environment.

Delicious invasive plant species you can forage in Texas include:

- Kudzu
- Alligator weed
- Bastard cabbage
- Chinese parasol tree
- Chinese tallow tree
- Water hyacinth
- Japanese honeysuckle
- Jerusalem cherry
- Japanese privet
- Chinese privet
- Paper mulberry

Before you harvest any invasive plant species, be sure that you understand exactly which parts of the plant are edible.

THE IMPACT OF FORAGING ON PLANTS

Apart from being a food source, plants serve a variety of uses to us human beings such as:

- Medicine
- A fuel source
- To build shelter
- To develop fibers to make cloth
- To create tools
- To create weapons
- As a poison
- As a hallucinogen

Early humans relied heavily on plants for all of these uses and more. But as time has passed, human beings have swayed from their dependence on all of these uses. It is a sign of how much we have lost touch with nature. We are removing ourselves from the precious circle of life and it shows. We lack the essential knowledge of the features and processes of life. We lack empathy for how our actions affect nature. We walk through gardens and trapeze through forests without feeling the wind or noticing the land or its wonders. We have stopped valuing nature and its provisions.

But foraging has given us the pathway to make that reconnection. And that reconnection can benefit both us and nature, whether the plants we forage are native or non-native species. Foraging can be done in a sustainable, ethical way that not only helps plants thrive but also helps control invasive growth. Why? Because of that connection that is felt with nature. There is an understanding that

allows you to appreciate the jelly you created from the beautyberries you picked. There is a tangible associate with the stir-fry you created after harvesting prickly pear. When you participate in such acts, you become part of the local ecological habitat. You help create balance and so, you nurture the growth of native species to help them help the rest of the natural environment. You also help that balance by tipping the scales when foraging more for invasive plant species than for native species. There are many ways to care and cater to nature as a forager and thus, have a positive impact on the plants that you forage.

Let's take a closer look at what these wild edible plants are, and what benefits are associated with them...

CHAPTER 3

NATURE'S GIFT – WILD EDIBLE PLANTS

Now that we have looked at what ethical foraging is and the potential benefits that it has for humans and wild plants, there is still a burning question – what is considered a wild plant, and what makes some edible and others not? This chapter dives into that discussion along with the advantages of eating wild foods versus cultivated foods and the major families of wild foods.

WHAT ARE WILD EDIBLE PLANTS?

As mentioned earlier, cultivated food is in many ways responsible for the human population boom that our planet has experienced over the last few decades. But with a growing population comes the problem of feeding everyone. More than 80% of the food we eat is sourced from plant life. Relying on cultivated food has placed a tremendous strain on Earth's resources and thus, we cannot sustain life as is or further growth in the population this way. Turning to wild foods with a mind for conservation and ethics is the way to go.

So, what determines what wild food is? After all, we cannot just indiscriminately pick wild plants and eat them all. There are three characteristics that a wild food must fulfill to be deemed that:

1) It must grow without cultivation practices imparted by humans. Such practices include soil preparation or manipulation, weeding, irrigation, and manuring. It stands to reason that the use of chemicals like pesticides and herbicides cannot be used to grow such plants.
2) The plant must be taken from the environment where it grew in nature to be consumed.
3) It must be safe to consume without negative health implications.

By the virtue of those qualities, this planet is teaming with wild flora fit for human consumption. Of the almost 400,000 species of plants that have been discovered on this planet, we only consume about 200 of those species. Therefore, there is still room to discover which of these other hundreds of thousands of plant species are edible. Indulging in wild foods also allows us to diversify our diets and thus, be healthier and ultimately happier. Currently, despite the many options we have in wild plants, the human population is mostly sustained by three crops – wheat, maize, and rice. These three plants account for more than half of all the protein and calories we consume. We are leaving so much nutrition on the table by not diverting more from these three cultivated plants.

Wild foods have a crucial component that makes them provide more nutrients than cultivated foods and that is the presence of Phytochemicals in their chemical makeup. These plant-produced chemicals protect the plant from disease and damage. They also benefit humans when they are consumed to:

- Regulate our hormones
- Fight cancers
- Reduce inflammation
- Function with healthier immune systems

These chemicals enforce the plant's protection by emitting an unpleasant smell, causing the plant to taste bitter or sprout thorns. These features help deter animals that might feast on them. But it is these same chemicals that afford us these benefits listed above.

Phytochemicals may be found in cultivated foods, but wild foods contain more variety of different types. Two major categories of phytochemicals that you will find in wild foods are carotenoids and polyphenols. Polyphenols can further be broken down into categories like flavanols and anthocyanins. Even these categories can be broken down further. Anthocyanins can be found in wild blueberries (and other wild foods that contain purple and blue pigments). These compounds are scientifically proven to:

- Improve blood sugar metabolism
- Improve blood cholesterol levels
- Reduce the risk of developing diseases like breast cancer and heart disease

Apart from the nutritional benefits, more advantages to eating wild foods include greater accessibility compared to cultivated foods. No matter where in the world you live, wild foods can be found. In your backyard, on the side of the unpaved road while you walk home from work, in a local park, in the small patch of trees just off the road from where you go to the gym… there is no shortage of places where you can find wild foods.

But as you begin this journey of foraging for wild plants, be sure to keep the hazards in mind. Never forage on private property without permission. Know the foraging laws of where you forage. Investigate the foraging location to ensure that it is safe from chemicals and pollution. Start with foraging small amounts to be familiar with plants and ethical, safe practices and never take more than you need.

MAJOR GROUPINGS OF WILD EDIBLE PLANTS

The sheer number of edible wild plants makes it hard to keep track of them all. Therefore, it was necessary to group them based on like characteristics. Thus, edible plants families are:

The Lily Family (*Liliaceae*)

These plants showcase showy flowers that have 6-segmented flowers and fruits with three capsules. Such fruits dry as they mature and split open to release their seeds. Examples of wild plants in this family include wild onions, wild garlic, and wild leeks.

The Purslane Family (*Portulacaceae*)

This family of wild plants is characterized by flowering succulents and short shrubs. Miner's lettuce is an example of such a wild plant.

The Rose Family (*Rosaceae*)

Members of this flowering wild family group tend to be small shrubs or small to medium sized trees. They are also generally woody plants. Examples are blackberries and raspberries.

The Heath Family (*Ericaceae*)

Features to help you identify members of this plant family include evergreen leaves that are twisted or alternate in pattern and flowers that contain both male and female parts. Flower characteristics are highly varied in this plant family. Members of this family include blueberries.

The Mustard Family (*Brassicaceae*)

This plant family contains plants with leaves that are simple and appear in opposite or alternate patterns, have woody, erect stems, and feature taproots. Annual and biennial plants can be found in this plant family. Watercress and shepherd's purse are wild plants belonging to this family.

The Mint Family (*Lamiaceae*)

These are flowering shrubs or herbs with 4-sided stems. The leaves can be twisted or arranged in an opposite pattern, and emit a distinct strong flavor when crushed. Wild mint belongs to this wild plant family group.

The Sunflower Family (*Asteraceae*)

Annual and perennial shrubs and herbs appear in this plant family. Their flowering features can be quite complicated with different shapes and sexual qualities. Dandelion and pineapple weed belong to this plant family.

The Nettle Family (*Urticaceae*)

Characteristics that link plants to this family include varied leaves, sap that is typically watery, both female and male flowers on the same plant, and stinging hair. Stinging nettle belongs to this plant family.

The Cattail Family (*Typhaceae*)

The members of this plant family are recognized by brownish, spike-like flowers and leaves with different faces on either side. Broad-leaved cattail are found in this plant family.

The Beech Family (*Fagaceae*)

This plant family contains trees or shrubs with simple leaves and small, unisex flowers. Beeches, chestnuts, and oaks are members of this plant family.

The Pine Family (*Pinaceae*)

Pine, hemlock, fir, and spruce are members of this plant family. Members are characterized by evergreen, needle-like leaves on trees or shrubs that produce resin, a thick sap. Older members tend to have a thick, deeply grooved bark.

CHAPTER 4

PARTS OF A PLANT – AN IDENTIFICATION GUIDE

Most plants are not wholly edible. Different parts of wild plants are fit for consumption. The first part of educating yourself on which of these parts are edible on particular plants is learning the general anatomy of plants. This chapter is your crash course on that. The edible parts of plants, along with their characteristics and functions, are:

Roots

These are the parts of the plant that are typically underground. They anchor the plant to the soil as well as absorb nutrients and water from the soil so that the plant can synthesize its food. Additionally, the root system of the plant serves as a food reserve. Sometimes roots grow vertically to facilitate the process of respiration. These roots are known as pneumatophores. Sometimes roots grow out of other parts of the plant, and these are known as adventitious roots.

Stem

Ranging in color from plant species to plant species, stems rise from the shoot system of a plant and grow aboveground normally. When stems initially rise out of seeds, they are weak and have difficulty standing straight, but they typically grow to become the sturdiest part of the plant, which in the case of trees is called the trunk. The trunk is covered by the thicker outer cover known as the bark. As a result of this, one of the stem's primary functions is to support the plant and keep it upright.

The stem is also the vegetative propagation system that transports water and nutrients back and forth between the roots and the rest of the plant's parts like the flowers, fruits, and leaves. The stem also stores food and helps in reproduction. It can also develop into a security system with modified protection tools like thorns and prickles. Some plants have modified stem systems that grow underground. Examples of such plants include ginger and potato.

Leaves

Leaves contain a substance known as chlorophyll and along with this compound, the leaves use water, carbon dioxide, and sunlight to create the plant's food. This process of food production is known as photosynthesis. Along with producing the plant's food, leaves have two other functions which are transpiration and, sometimes, reproduction. Transpiration allows the plant to remove excess water from pores known as stomata. In the case of reproduction, sometimes leaves give rise to new leaves such as with the plant known as Bryophyllum.

The structure of the leaf blade is made up of three main parts known as the lamina, leaf base, and petiole. The lamina is the structure that contains the veins that keep the leaf rigid so that it is able to transport water and nutrients. The leaf base keeps the plant anchored to the branch or stem so that it protrudes from the rest of the plant. The petiole allows the leaf to keep cool.

Flowers

These are the main reproductive parts of the plant. They contain four main parts known as the petals, sepals, stamen, and pistil. The petals are colorful and vary in size and shape from flower to flower. Their main purpose is to attract insects and birds to the flowers so that pollination is facilitated. The sepals are a green, leafy part underneath the petals. They protect the flower from damage. The stamens are the male part of the flower and contain the smaller segments known as the anther and filament. The pistils are the female part of the flower and contain the smaller components known as the ovary, style, and stigma.

Fruits

These are a product of plants that flower. They are typically the mature ovary that forms after the successful pollination of flowers. In instances where fruits are produced without fertilization facilitated by pollination, the fruit is called parthenocarpy or parthenocarpic. Examples of such fruits include pineapple and banana. Such fruits are seedless.

IDENTIFICATION METHODS

These parts are what will help you identify wild plants successfully as they vary in appearance from plant to plant. One might have toothed leaves while another has smooth edges. Where one plant has small roots that do not venture far from the plant, another might have swollen roots called tubers that hold the vast majority of a plant's food and nutrition. I can go on and on listing the ways that plant features can vary. However, the thing I want to impress upon you is that positive identification is a matter of safety. False identification can lead to poisoning, something we will discuss in the next chapter.

There are a few ways that you can develop your skills of identification and they are:

Plant Hike with an "Expert"

This is a beginner-friendly way of becoming familiar with plants, as it allows you to pick the brain of a professional forager. This person can point out features and plants that you might not have noticed on your own as someone who does not yet know what to look for when practicing this skill. This makes you more aware of how much it pays to be mindful on your harvesting trips. Sometimes, a human touch makes all the difference in how easily you retain information.

There are many ways that you can get in touch with an expert forager. For example, there are local communities of foragers who go on hikes together. You can join such groups and gain guidance from several experts at once. There are also online communities that you can become a part of where experts are ready and available to help you and also plan trips in the wild.

If you are unable to sync calendars with an expert, you can take a trip on your own and use online resources and discussions with experts to identify plants. All you have to do is take a picture and share it in the most helpful form such as on social media groups or through direct messaging with an expert to confirm the identity of a plant.

Field Guide ID in the Field

Field guides are books and online resources that allow you to identify plants with descriptions, photos, and sometimes illustrations. It pays to pick up a few of these so that you can identify plants not only by their features but also by how they relate to each other in plant families.

Patterns-Method of Plant ID

This is the most labor-intensive of the three identification methods,

but one of the most rewarding for people who plan to become professional foragers. You need to apply methods of study so that you mentally retain patterns that allow you to identify plants in the wild. Not only will you learn the characteristics of plant families, but you will also link plants by specific properties. This study will also allow you to become more familiar with the different uses of various plants.

One of the most popular patterns through which foragers identify plants appears via their leaves. Leaves have different characteristics such as shape, color, fragrance, form, and edges. It helps to take two different types of leaves and note the differences in their characteristics.

In my opinion, you should not limit yourself to one form of plant identification. Hiking with experts allows you to socialize with and learn from someone like-minded yet with more experience. Field guilds allow you to feel instant gratification with learning and the patterns-method gains you the mental stimulation necessary for long-term advancement as a forager.

THE METHODOLOGY FOR IDENTIFYING PLANTS

Identifying plants can be a daunting task with the risk of poisoning looming over your head. Do not let the anxiety of such a potential occurrence keep you from enjoying your foraging adventure. You do not have to throw caution to the wind to do so, either. There is a systematic way of approaching plant identification that will let your mind rest easy as you forage. The first step in this system is guessing. That's right! Based on what you have learned about plants in your area, you need to make an educated guess on what you think a plant is.

Once you have a list of the plants you think this might be, it is time

to narrow things down with a comparison reference. This means inspecting the plant carefully to note its characteristics and then comparing it to the features listed for the potential suspect in your field guides. Ensure that these characteristics match what is described in the field guides. Never try to force the issue if a feature does not line up. Run through the features listed by at least 3 field guides for cross-reference. Do not touch the plant until you have a positive ID confirmation.

Lastly, look for more samples. The exact environment that a plant lives in changes how it grows. For example, if your sample was growing in a space where the soil composition matches its needs exactly and it is getting the right amount of sunlight and water, it will look healthy compared to the same plant growing in a space where a nutrient it needs is lacking in the soil and if it has to fight with other plants to get adequate sunlight and water. The latter plant might have yellow-tinged leaves or a less rigid stem. You need to be able to spot the differences that will occur with these nuances in conditions. Do not rush this process. It will likely take a few hours as you inspect that environment but it will also be ongoing when you learn to do this inspection as you come across the plant in future forages.

As you gain more experience with foraging and plant identification, your confidence will grow as you learn to recognize plants. This confidence will have you positively IDing plants even when someone else contradicts the identification of your find. When you have this deep-seated self-assurance in your abilities, that is when you can start consuming your finds in the wild. If there is ever any doubt in a plant's ID, simply observe and continue to develop your powers of identification.

ON-THE-GO RESOURCES

No matter how much knowledge you acquire beforehand, it is easy to get confused when faced with the many plants in nature. That is why it is so important that you go on foraging trips with multiple guides. Carrying many physical books can become tedious and tiring, though. Luckily, technology is on your side. Your smartphone can be used as an invaluable resource, allowing you to access many websites that aid with plant identification. A few of these websites include:

- PLANTS Database (Natural Resources Conservation Service) - plants.usda.gov
- Lady Bird Johnson Wildflower Center (University of Texas at Austin) - wildflower.org/
- PFAF Database (Plants for a Future) - pfaf.org/
- National Invasive Species Information Center – U.S. Dept. of Agriculture. invasivespeciesinfo.gov
- https://identify.plantnet.org (This has an app for smartphones, both Android and iOS)
- https://unitedplantsavers.org/species-at-risk-list (This website shows plant species at risk list so that you can avoid harvesting them)
- USDA database - https://plants.sc.egov.usda.gov/home
- https://gobotany.nativeplanttrust.org/simple/ (This website has a simple key to follow and narrow down plant ID)

Your phone, this lightweight compact tool, also allows you to access digital books, podcasts, and videos on the go. Both Android and iOS devices also allow the installation of apps that help with plant ID as well.

With foraging wild plants come the risks of walking into something unknown that can be potentially harmful. It's time to factor in your safety in these adventures.

CHAPTER 5

THE MATTERS OF SAFETY

With the many advantages and the great wonders of being so close to nature, it is easy to forget that foraging does come with a particular set of dangers. One such danger is the risk of becoming poisoned by coming into contact with particular plant parts or consuming toxic wild plants. Safety needs to be at the forefront of your mind as a forager. This might seem like an obvious thing but the statistics show many unsuspecting foragers have to deal with the repercussions of not following this simple rule - **Never consume or touch any wild plant that you cannot absolutely identify**.

In addition, you need to positively confirm that the area that you are foraging in is safe to do so. An otherwise edible plant can become inedible due to growing in an area that has been polluted by human activity. Forage in areas that have as little human population as possible. Do not forage in spaces close to busy roadsides, industrial areas, and other sources of potential human pollution.

It can be quite difficult to keep track of poisonous plants in addition to edible plants as a beginner forager, but you do not have to know every poisonous plant in order to avoid them. What you do have to know is exactly what wild plans you are eating.

Plants that are typically safe to eat include:

- Tree nuts. These are plentiful in North American woodlands and are full of calories being healthy sources of fat and protein. They are typically hard to crack into as they have an outer husk and an inner shell that protects the inner meat. As a rule of thumb, be sure that this inner meat looks veiny. Stay away from nuts with inner meat that looks smooth and rounded. Examples of tree nuts that are safe to consume include pecan, hickory nuts, pine nuts, and even acorns.

- Familiar berries. Not all berries are created safe to eat but there is a wide variety of those that grow in the wild that you can pick fresh off the branch, wash off, and snack on. Stick to easily recognizable wild berries such as raspberries, elderberries, beautyberries, and blackberries. Avoid all white berries as these tend to be poisonous.

- Uproot aquatic plants. Near wetlands, rivers, and lakes are typical locations where you can find edible wild plants, particularly the roots of these plants. These roots tend to be a great source of protein, fiber, and carbohydrates. They tend to need cooking because of this highly fibrous nature. Common edible wild plants of this nature include cattail and bulrush.

If there is ever a time that you run into a wild plant that you are interested in chowing down on but you are not sure of its edibility, do not turn away immediately in disappointment. You can determine its edibility with the universal edibility test.

THE UNIVERSAL EDIBILITY TEST

The universal edibility test is the process of taking small amounts of a plant and increasing contact with that plant over time to determine if there are any negative effects of consuming that plant. This is a test that you should limit to emergency survival situations. In fact, it was originally developed by the US Army to help soldiers identify potential edible food sources in the wild. It is not one to be used to identify edible wild plants right away.

A quick rundown of how to perform the universal edibility test includes the following steps:

1. Smell the plant part. If the plant smells like a rotting corpse or emits any other awful scent, throw it away and stop the test.

2. If the plant part does not smell bad, hold it against your wrist or inner elbow for 15 minutes. If there is itching, burning, or any other adverse reaction, throw it away and stop the test.

3. If there is no adverse reaction to your skin, place the plant part against your lips for 15 minutes. If there is itching, burning, or any other adverse reaction, throw it away and stop the test.

4. If there is no adverse reaction against your lips, take a pea-sized bite of this plant part. While you should not expect that most plant part tastes like they have been prepared in a 5-star restaurant, if the plant part tastes soapy or bitter, spit it out immediately and wash out your mouth. If the taste of the plant part is bearable hold the bite in your mouth for 15 minutes.

5. If after 15 minutes there is not an adverse reaction, chew the small bite and swallow. Wait for at least 6 hours and if at that point you do not feel sick or have any other adverse reaction, then the plant part is likely safe to eat.

Note that each plant part deserves a separate universal edibility test.

So, if you test out the roots in one trial, you need to do a separate test for the leaves, flowers, stems, etc. The universal edibility test is particularly useful in survival situations such as if you got lost in the woods. Even if that extreme situation does not occur, it is highly useful to know the universal edibility test.

IDENTIFY POISONOUS PLANTS

A poisonous plant is considered to cause harmful effects via contact or ingestion. These poisonous effects can be particularly dangerous for people who already have certain allergies or sensitivities such as dermatitis. While it is easier to err on the side of identifying edible plants, it is also useful for you to know the typical characteristics of poisonous plants that you might encounter out in the wild. Such characteristics include:

- Milky sap. This is one of the most common characteristics of plants that are toxic for consumption and to have contact with. Contact with them can irritate the eyes and skin. Ingesting them can cause symptoms such as vomiting and nausea. Parts of the milkweed release a milky sap.

- White and yellow berries. They typically look like doll eyes and are very attractive. Consuming them can cause symptoms like vomiting, diarrhea, and nausea. Nightshade has such berries.

- Dull-looking or glossy green leaves. These leaves typically come in patterns such as in threes, have toothed edges, and are smooth. Examples include poison ivy and poison sumac.

- A single leaf with 3 leaflets. Poison ivy is an example of this. These three leaflets in one leaf make it so that one of these leaves is upright and the other two sit on the left and right sides of this.

- Umbel-shaped plant parts. The leaves and flowers and other plant parts are shaped like umbrellas. Water hemlock is an example of a poisonous plant with this particular characteristic.

It should be noted that not every single plant that displays the characteristics listed above is poisonous. However, it is better to err on the side of caution rather than ignore these characteristics. We will discuss a few typical examples of poisonous plants that you will encounter while foraging in Texas later in this book.

If you ever suspect that you have been poisoned, reach out to Poison Control USA by calling 1-800-222-1222 (https://www.poison.org/).

TOOLS AND SAFETY EQUIPMENT

Being a safe forager is not just about the plants that you come into contact with and eat, or having the knowledge of whether plants are edible or poisonous. It is also about the equipment, tools, and gear that you use for foraging. Using the right items makes the experience not only more enjoyable but also more productive while increasing the probability that you will remain safe during your adventures.

A list of items that you should have in your forager's tool kit includes:

- Multiple field guides to help you identify plants on the go. Ensure that these field guides help the identification process with vivid descriptions, illustrations, and photos.

- Garden shovels for digging up edible wild plant parts that are underground.

- Digging fork, also for digging up edible wild plant parts are on the ground

- A pruning knife, which is a hooked-shaped knife for cutting away vines and stalks in a single stroke.

- Pruning shears for cutting harder to slice branches and stalks.
- Pruning saw for cutting small to medium tree branches and stems.
- A folding knife to use as an easy-to-access cutting tool.
- Gloves to protect your hands.
- Long-sleeved shirt and pants to protect your arms and legs.
- A hat to protect your head.
- Waterproof boots.
- Breathable bags for storing wild plants.
- Assorted baskets for carrying and storing wild plant foods.
- Hand lens for making small plant part identification easier.
- First aid kit.
- A backpack for easy carrying of harvested foods and forager must-haves.
- A noisemaker to deter dangerous wildlife.
- A map, GPS device, and compass to help you find your way.
- A journal to keep notes on plants and conditions.

The last few chapters have discussed how you should identify edible wild plants sustainably and ethically while being safe during foraging. It is time to venture into the territory of where you can find to forage for edible wild plants in Texas and the particular wild plants that you will find there. Let's hop right into the next part of this book!

PART – II

Foraging In Texas

CHAPTER 6

LAWS OF THE LAND

Every place on this planet has specific rules about what can be foraged and how this should be done. Texas is no different. While the act of foraging itself might make you feel that you can access free food in any form or capacity, there are certain laws that you must obey, which change from state to state within the United States of America. This chapter outlines the specifics of those in Texas so that your foraging adventures remain within the confines of the law.

FORAGING RULES IN TEXAS

For you to ensure that you follow Texan foraging laws, you need to communicate with others. That might seem daunting to introverts, but I assure you that once like-minded individuals get together, the conversation is always stimulating. You need to engage in this conversation because one of the most important laws governing foragers in Texas is that no plant material can be harvested on property that is not your own without the expressed permission from the owner. I look at this as an opportunity to bond with other foragers and nature-lovers and I hope that you do, too.

There are particular laws regulating foraging in Texan forests, national parks, historic sites, and state parks, as well. You must investigate the specifics of each area.

A list of some of the Texan State parks that you should become familiar with include:

- Big Bend Ranch State Park
- Davis Mountains State Park
- Fairfield Lake State Park
- Guadalupe River State Park
- Texas State Park

A few national parks to add to that list are:

- Big Bend National Park
- Guadalupe Mountains National Park
- Lyndon B. Johnson National Historical Park

And don't forget the state forests of Fairchild State Forest and WG Jones State Forest and the national forests of Angelina National Forest, Davy Crockett National Forest, Sabine National Forest, and Sam Houston National Forest.

These areas do not allow commercial harvesting. Some of these areas do not allow the picking or uprooting of wildflowers, even for personal use. This is typically the case when these flowers grow in council parks or community gardens.

Some areas have regulations on the amount of a wild plant part that may be harvested. For example, make note that some areas do not allow more than one gallon of berries or nuts to be harvested per family. Most US National Forests including in Texas allow the picking of fruits and nuts. In fact, most national parks and forests do not take offense to the sustainable foraging of the Four Fs, which are fruit, foliage, fungi, or flowers as long as they are for personal use.

Texas Edible Wild Plant Foraging

On the flip side, it is an offense to uproot any plant.

If you are ever in doubt about if a wild plant can be harvested, simply leave it be until you can get the right information surrounding its harvesting.

FORAGING DO'S AND DON'TS IN TEXAS

Do's

- Do learn the ins and outs of Texan foraging laws to ensure you are helping sustain nature in the state. It is also necessary knowledge to gain since Texan laws are rather strict in that regard.
- Do respect nature, yourself as a forager, and other foragers by abiding by the laws and regulations that govern Texas and any other state that you might forage in. Foraging does not mean picking what nature has at just any time or without discrimination. It means doing so mindfully and respectfully.
- Do gain permission before foraging on private property to not only respect the owner's claim but also to avoid penalties and fees. This can lead to physical harm and danger if you do otherwise as it is not unheard of for property owners to protect their property with firearms.
- Forage only what you need so that nature can sustain itself and so that other foragers can also benefit from what nature provides.
- Do always positively identify wild plants before touching or eating them.
- Do be patient as you learn to forage. This is not a skill that is mastered overnight. It takes years to become a seasoned professional.
- Do limit the range of the location that you forage so that you

maintain the sustainability of the practice.

- Do forage wild plants that are found commonly around Texas such as:
    - Mulberries
    - Mexican Plums
    - Rosemary
    - Pecans
    - Pomegranates
    - Hackberries

Don'ts

- Do not harvest wild plants that fall under the endangered plants' list. This list includes:
    - American Chaffseed (*Schwalbea americana*)
    - Bald Cypress (*Taxodium distichum*)
    - Butterfly Weed (*Asclepias tuberosa*)
    - Cardinal Flower (*Lobelia cardinalis*)
    - Earth Fruit (*Geocarpon minimum*)
    - Flowering Dogwood (*Cornus florida*)
    - Maximilian Sunflower (*Helianthus maximiliani*)

    For more information on the threatened and endangered plant (and animal) species list in Texas (and to keep abreast as to when and if this changes), visit https://tpwd.texas.gov/

- Do not destroy, remove, or dig up any plant life.
- Do not gather wild plants outside of the areas designated to do so.
- Do not forage for commercial purposes.

As you forage, you have to be ethical in your ways (see chapter 2-A) while also taking care to keep true to the laws of Texas. Be sure that you do not end up foraging for a wild plant that is protected by the

Texas Edible Wild Plant Foraging

state or by the owner of private property. Whenever you are in doubt, seek permission and more information. It is better to air on the side of caution.

Now, with all these rules and regulations in hindsight, where can you forage within Texas? Continue reading to find out.

CHAPTER 7

WHERE TO FORAGE IN TEXAS?

As we have gotten the "Lay of the Land" of Texas rules and regulations wise and discussed how you can ethically forage within the state's borders, it is time to tell you exactly where in Texas you can start your adventures.

RURAL FORAGING IN TEXAS

The most obvious place to forage in Texas is in its natural habitat. The specific wild plant life that you will find in these areas varies from place to place due to factors such as the diversity of soil types, the particular climate of those areas, the frequency of rainfall, and more. For example, you will find more humid conditions in East Texas and so, trees like bay laurel are frequent finds. On the other hand, West Texas has more desert-like conditions and cacti like cow's tongue and prickly pear are common sights. Northern Texas is famous for its grassy plains and therefore, you will find Texas dandelions and dayflowers in such areas in abundance.

The main natural habitats that you will find ideal for foraging in Texas include:

Texas Edible Wild Plant Foraging

Piney Woods

These are on the Eastern borders of Texas and occupy about 16 million acres. As the title suggests, large amounts of timber trees such as pine, oak, hickory, and elm grow in this area. Typical plants for foraging that can be found in that area include Indian grass, bluestems, magnolia, panicums, and blackseed needlegrass.

Gulf Prairies and Marshes

This occupies the southeastern part of Texas, covering approximately 10 million acres. Popular forage items in this area include weeds and grass-like red lovegrass, Indian grass, switchcane, and dayflowers.

Post Oak Savannah

This borders the piney woods areas and goes further inland. It is a secondary forest area of the pine woods area and covers about 7 million acres. Rainfall is less frequent and this area has a higher elevation. It also grows many timber trees like oak and elm in addition to trees that demand lots of water like walnuts and pecans. It also features popular forageable grasses like Indian grass, bullnettle, and red love grass.

Blackland Prairies

Approximately 12 million acres long, this area borders the Post Oak Savannah on its eastern end and encroaches on the mid-Texan territory. There is less grass vegetation and more plants. Timber trees like oak and elm are found often along streams. This area is highly cultivated and pasteurized but a few of the wild plants that can be frequently foraged include Texas wintergrass and Indian grass.

Cross Timbers and Prairies

This starts on the Eastern end of the Blackland Prairies and moves further east. It occupies approximately 15 million acres and has a mixture of prairies and woodlands. There's a sharp contrast to the vegetation that grows there compared to the areas previously mentioned because of the typography and the soil types that are found in this area. However, woody vegetation such as oaks and grasses such as Indian grass can be foraged in such areas.

South Texas Plains

As the name tells, this occupies South Texas. It is about 21 million acres and has more desert-like conditions. As a result, cactus-like prickly pear are frequently found and foraged. Grasses, weeds, small trees, and woody shrubs can also be found and foraged there, as well.

Edwards Plateau

This area occupies space from southwest to Central Texas and is about 25 million acres. The vegetation there is a mixture of small trees, weeds, and grasses because of the soil composition, which is limestone-based.

Rolling Plains

This bothers North to Central Texas and is about 24 million acres. This area is a mixture of woodlands and prairies and features coarse sands and clay beds. The weather is also dryer and therefore, plants that can survive in arid conditions like yucca can be found in this area.

High Plains

This is on the northwest end borders of Texas and is approximately 19 million acres. Trees are not a frequent sight because of the porous soil and low rainfall rates. Yucca and cacti grow well in such conditions.

Trans-Pecos Mountains and Basins

This sits on the western end of Texas and occupies about 18 million acres of land. Conditions are dry and this area experiences as little as 8 inches of rain a year. Grass is not a frequent sight and if it is sighted, it is short and scattered. Wild plants that thrive in this area include yucca and the cactus-like prickly pear.

URBAN FORAGING IN TEXAS

It might not seem like it but our city jungles can be just as fruitful as natural habitats for finding edible wild plants. Texas is no exception. Foraging in such habitats is known as urban foraging. While urban centers do not provide miles and miles of land like those mentioned above, if you know where to look your spoils can be plentiful. For you to gain such an advantage, you need to understand the Texan cities and towns where you live. Take time to walk around the area and familiarize yourself with back alleys, streams, parks, and other areas that are off the beaten path.

Using city maps is also a way to help you become familiar with the "unbeaten paths" where you live. There are even apps that allow you to pinpoint a specific location of harvestable wild plants in your area. One such app is known as *Falling Fruit* and it helps users pinpoint where they can find such wild foods in public areas like parks and near fences. So if you have a craving for wild onions in urban Texas, be sure to look up such an app to find directions on how you can find them.

Prime habitats for urban foraging include:

Walls, fences, and boundary edges

These areas often replicate natural habitats because they are often undisturbed. Therefore, plant life tends to thrive there and so, forageable wild foods typically grow abundantly. Passion vines and

other creeping plants can often be found in such areas, as they use their grabbing abilities to hold onto such structures to grow.

Woodlands and copses (small groups of trees)

Urban areas are not completely absent of vegetative areas. There are a few woodland areas and copses that can be found around urban Texan borders. These are prime places to find grass, weeds, and berries.

Chalk and Limestone Grassland Plants

Such areas were typically forested in the past but human settling cleared out the area of vegetation largely. However, the semi-natural area is still one where plant life grows. Examples of such plants you can find around Texas include yarrow, Queen Anne's lace, and Indian strawberry.

Urban foraging by streams, rivers, and estuaries

Plantlife is always attracted to water no matter where it is. Therefore, streams, rivers, and other water bodies are prime places to find forageable wild plants. Duckweed, alligator weed, and dayflower are common sights in such areas.

Coastal areas

The area where land meets the coast in Texas towns such as Galveston and Freeport are abundant with thriving wild plants.

Wastegrounds

Not every single piece of land is being used by humans in urban spaces. There are often large pieces of neglected and uncultivated land where vegetation grows and is untampered with. These are prime places to forage.

Disturbed ground, cracks, and crevices

Many of the plants that we see as weeds growing through cracks,

crevices, and other places that are disturbed by human beings possess hidden wild goodies. Examples of such goodies that you can find in Texas include amaranth and bastard cabbage.

Cemeteries, parks, and public gardens

Yarrow, dandelions, nasturtium, bullnettle, and beautyberries are just a few of the edible wild plants that you can find in such areas in Texas. This is because these areas are dedicated to allowing plant life to thrive.

WHERE NOT TO FORAGE IN TEXAS

As important as it is to know where to forage, it is equally as important to know what areas you should avoid. Scouting where you live gives you an idea of the places that you can go to forage and those that you should avoid. Your foraging plan with every outing should list such cases. Such areas are typically in urban environments due to the higher risk of contamination and oil, and water through pollution. However, you should also avoid areas that are known to have dangerous wildlife or are precarious when foraging in natural habitats.

A quick list of areas that you should consider danger zones for foraging include:

- Areas that are sprayed with pesticides and herbicides such as the borders of farms
- Near busy roadways, auto shops, industrial plants, factories, gas stations, and other commercialized areas
- Parking lots
- On private property without permission
- Under power lines and other utility appliances
- Manicured and landscaped public spaces

No matter where you forage, be sure to positively ID a plant with at

least three characteristics before harvest in it.

RULES FOR FORAGING

No matter where you forage, whether in a natural habitat or urban settings, here are 5 rules that you should always follow to ensure safe, healthy, and ethical adventures:

1. Forage with friends to develop those interpersonal connections as well as to be safer during outings
2. Forage in spots where chemicals are not used
3. Always positively identify a plant before harvesting
4. Follow the rules of the areas that you are foraging in. There are federal, state, and city laws that govern every single area where you might seek to forage so familiarize yourself with these
5. Understand times of year best for foraging wild plants that you particularly enjoy to ensure safe, efficient, and productive foraging trips

This chapter has answered the *where* to forage in Texas but *what* do you forage in Texas? The next chapter answers that question.

CHAPTER 8

WHAT TO FORAGE IN TEXAS?

With where to forage in Texas out of the way, let's dive into the what of it all. It is easier to create a mental catalog of the things that are safe to consume rather than those you should avoid so that is what this chapter aims to do – arm you with a list of edible wild plants found in Texas. We will expand on the characteristics of some of the plants in Directory 1 in PART III of the book.

FAQS ABOUT WILD EDIBLE PLANTS FOUND IN TEXAS

What are some of the most popular wild edible plants found in Texas?

Some of the most popular wild edible plants found across Texas natural and urban habitats are:

- Texas dandelion
- Wild onion
- Bullnettle
- Elderberry
- Wild Raspberry
- Garlic Mustard

- Pecans
- Yucca
- Wireweed
- Spiderwort
- Sheep sorrel
- Chickweed

What are some wild plants native to Texas?

Some native plants found in the Texan wild include:

- Cactus like prickly pear and cow's tongue.
- Berries like southern dewberry and beautyberry.
- Peppers like Chile pequin.
- Succulents like yucca, agave, purslane, and Texas stonecrop.
- Flowers like dandelion and winecup.
- Wild veggies like Queen Ann's lace, wild onion, bastard cabbage, and sweet potatoes.
- Nuts and seeds like pecan and seed pods from redbud.

What wild edible plants grow in Central Texas?

Wild edible plants found in Central Texas include:

- Beautyberry
- Passion vine
- Frog fruit
- Live oak
- Strawberry cactus
- Spiderwort
- Mexican plum

What plants can you forage in East Texas?

Berries are quite the popular foraging find in East Texas and so you can harvest:

- Dewberries

Texas Edible Wild Plant Foraging

- Wild blackberries
- Mulberries
- Huckleberries
- Indian strawberries
- Farkleberries
- Beautyberries

More wild plants that can be foraged in East Texas include:

- Pimpernel
- Wild onion
- Magnolia
- Lizard's tail
- Live oak
- Queen Anne's Lace
- Kudzu
- Canna Lily

What berries grow wild in Texas?

Quite a few berries can be foraged in Texas and that list includes:

- Dewberries
- Mexican plums
- Wild blackberries
- Mulberries
- Wild blueberries
- Huckleberries
- Indian strawberries
- Farkleberries
- Texas persimmon
- Beautyberries
- Woodland strawberry

What are the common edible plants of Hill County?

Commonly found edible wild plants of Hill County include:

- Acorns
- Common persimmon
- Texas persimmon
- Agarita
- Prickly pear
- Mustang Grapes
- Woodland strawberry
- Mexican plum
- Turk's Cap
- Creek plum
- Dewberry

Can you eat clover in Texas?

Clovers are found most commonly in the Post Oak Savanah and Piney Woods regions in Texas. Many of its parts are edible. That includes its young leaves, flowers, and seeds. The flowers can be used to make tea while the seeds can be eaten raw or roasted to be ground into flour, which I love to use to make porridge.

Where are dandelions found in Texas?

Dandelion can be found scattered across Texas but it is most commonly found in west to central Texas.

What wild fruits are native to Texas?

Some Texan native edible wild fruits are:

- Pawpaw
- Flatwoods Plum
- Dewberries
- Mulberries
- Prickly pear
- Western mayhaw
- Mustang grapes

Texas Edible Wild Plant Foraging

What plant leaves are edible in Texas?

Plants with edible leaves found in Texas include:

- Alligator weed
- Amaranth
- Bay laurel
- Dayflower
- Duckweed
- Frog fruit
- Gingko
- Indian strawberry
- Japanese hawkweed
- Kudzu
- Lizard's tail
- Lady's thumb
- Magnolia
- Nasturtium
- Wild onion
- Passion vine
- Pimpernel
- Pineapple weed
- Sheep sorrel
- Spiderwort
- Sweet potato
- Texas dandelion
- Wine cup
- Wireweed
- Yarrow

What are some edible succulents in Texas?

Edible succulents in Texas include:

- Yucca
- Agave

- Purslane
- Chisme
- Texas stonecrop

What are some edible cacti in Texas?

Cactus is quite the edible delight in Texas, so much so that the prickly pear cactus was named the state plant in 1995. Other edible cacti include:

- Cow's tongue
- Cholla Cactus
- Barrel Cactus

What can you do with the edible plants that you find? Harvest them, of course! But the question is – how do you do that? Let's dive deep into the rich world of harvesting edible plants and storing them for long-term use next.

CHAPTER 9

HOW TO HARVEST EDIBLE PLANTS

Let me lay out the scenario for you. You've set up your gear and have got everything ready to explore the wilderness. You have packed your bags, tied your shoelaces tight, and you even have your long-sleeved clothes to ensure you don't brush your bare skin against something poisonous like poison ivy. You are looking and feeling the part of a champion forager. You are ready to venture into the wild to forage.

You set out onto the unbeaten path and 15 minutes in, you spot an interesting-looking shrub with dark clumps of small, round berries. You use your identifying skills or message an expert about it, and come to the conclusion that these are elderberries! That's a successful forage, especially since you have just 100% positively IDed the plant part before even touching it. Remember to never take a chance with a plant that you have not identified!

But is it really a successful foraging mission?

The very term "forage" means in part to search, and that is what you have done. But, what now? How do you want to consume these berries? Maybe take them home and make something delicious out of them? Or perhaps, eat them right away?

Whether you use these berries now or later, the fact is that you have to pick them from the tree without damaging them. You could just wing it, but that is an unsustainable and unethical practice that can damage the plant and prevent yourself and other foragers from benefiting from the plant in the future.

So winging it is definitely not an option. There are techniques to ensure that, when done right, a plant will continue to grow and won't be damaged despite you harvesting it. Let's explore what these methods are by individual plant parts.

HARVESTING LEAVES AND GREENS

To harvest leaves ethically and encourage new growth, engage in the act of pinching. Pinching is the process of removing the upper portion of a leaf stem so that new leaf growth is encouraged from lower dormant leaf buds. You will find this dormant leaf bud where the leaf meets the stem, indicated by a small knob. As long as this knob is there, lower leaves will not grow. But when you remove this knob when harvesting the leaves, you signal to the plant not only to produce a new leaf, but likely two since dormant leaf buds typically come in pairs. Therefore, when you pinch one leaf, you encourage the growth of two new ones to take its place. The plant grows healthier and bigger because of your actions.

Pinching involves the action of holding the top of the leaf stem between your thumb and pointer finger so that the top part gets removed neatly. Only pinch when the plant is still young or if you are not taking many leaves from the plant.

HARVESTING GREENS

Some of my favorite greens found in Texas are the dandelion and bullnettles. With such greens, all you have to do to harvest is engage in pinching. Do this when the plants are less than 6" and only remove the top portion of leaves.

With other greens like chickweed, which normally appears in winter and the early spring on many lawns across Texas, harvest these by using sharp scissors or pruning shears to snip off the top part of the stem along with its leaves since the entire portion is edible.

Leaf buds should be harvested in the same way.

HARVESTING LEAF SHOOT / LEAF STALK "SPEARS"

Leaf shoots are spear-like items that appear as the new leaves of some plants. The leaf and the stalk are typically edible in such cases and we treat such finds like celery, feasting on both parts. An example of such plants found in Texas is hogweed. Harvest these before they flower, as you would greens like chickweed.

HARVESTING STEMS

You do not want to kill off a plant when you harvest its stem. There is a proper method for ensuring that this does not happen. Use a sharp knife or pruning shear to cut above a node where possible. This will allow new growth as a dormant bud will spring up. To harvest the entire stem, cut it at ground level before the plant flowers.

HARVESTING THE WHOLE PLANT

If you are harvesting the entire plant, do so before it flowers by gently uprooting and shaking the roots free of the soil.

HARVESTING BARKS

Harvesting of this plant part typically occurs in spring. This is because the sap of the plant rises at that time and makes the bark easier to pull away from the tree. Normally, the branches from which the bark will be harvested must be between three and five years old. Woody trees give away their age with the number of scars on the branch. These scars arise when buds burst annually. To harvest bark, all you have to do is cut it away. Do not remove bark from the plant's trunk. Also, do not peel away bark from branches in complete circles.

HARVESTING FLOWERS

Flowers like nasturtium have a peppery flavor and can be eaten and used to make beverages like teas. Such flowers should be harvested in the early morning before the day gets too hot or late in the afternoon after the heat of the day is fading away. These are the times when the flowers have still retained their moisture best. Do not pick flowers that are not completely open or those that have started wilting. Gently pick the flowers and place them in a basket or similar container that will ensure the flowers do not get squashed. Clean the flowers gently to remove any dirt or bug then refrigerate the flowers until you are prepared to use them.

When it is time for use, wash the flowers and remove the productive parts so that the flavor of the flowers is not affected. Some people are also allergic to these parts so it is doubly important to get rid of

them. Be sure that the remaining parts of the flowers are edible before you use them. For example, only the petals of a yucca flower are edible so the rest of the flower cannot be used.

HARVESTING FLOWER BUDS

Harvest flower buds like dandelions when they are firm and as young as possible. Do so in the mornings just before they have fully opened and before it has rained. Pinch them off. If the flower buds grow in clusters like they do with yarrow plants, use a sharp knife or pruning shears to cut off the stalk and then snip off the flowers after. Always remove the green matter on the flower buds before you use them.

HARVESTING SEEDS AND NUTS

Seeds are edible parts of a plant encased with a coat while nuts are technically hard-shelled fruits. Seeds are found within fruit. If the fruits are fleshy, then you need to wait until the fruit is ripe to obtain the mature seeds. After you have harvested the fruits, slice them open and shake the dry seeds free in the case of fruits that resemble peppers. With fruit that has pulp like tomatoes, remove the pulp and place it in a container of water. The seeds will sink to the bottom and pulp will rise. Stir this mixture once a day until the two items are completely free from each other. Remove the pulp and strain the seeds. Next, place the seeds on a towel to dry out. You can use them as desired after. For seeds from dry fruit, break open the fruits and shake the seeds free.

When a plant has a seed head, place the structure in a paper bag and shake to separate the seeds from the rest of the plant matter. Simply remove the seeds after.

HARVESTING ROOTS

The typical times for harvesting roots are spring and fall. During spring, roots are coming away from winter frost and this catalyzes the processes that convert their carbohydrates into simple sugar, so they taste sweeter. In fall, the plants are pulling in nutrition in preparation for winter dormancy and so their flavor is amazing.

Harvesting roots properly depends on the type of root. For tap roots (tubers) like sweet potatoes, you need to dig and put in a little elbow grease to get to it. Fibrous roots are easier to access. All you have to do is dig a small circle around the base of the plant and gently shake the roots free. Roots from biennial plants (plants that complete their life cycle over two growing seasons) need to be harvested in their first year of growth. Perennial plants grow for 3 or more growing seasons. You harvest some of these roots at a time so that the plant keeps on growing. You should try to limit harvesting to once a year during spring or fall.

HARVESTING FRUIT

How fruit is properly harvested depends on the type of fruit in question. Dry fruits such as those that have seed pods with nuts and seeds insides should be pinched away from the stem. Fleshy fruit should be harvested by gently twisting the stem away from the rest of the plants so that you do not impede future growth. Berries grow in clusters and, in this case, you should cut off the whole stem and then strip it off the fruits later. This will happen easily when the berries are ripe.

HARVESTING CACTI

Cacti have a variety of parts that can be harvested such as the leaves

Texas Edible Wild Plant Foraging

and flowers, but the plant part of particular interest in this section is the cactus pads. They can be eaten raw at times. The inner meat of these can be used to make jams and jellies. They can sometimes be used as meat substitutes. Cacti, like cow's tongue and prickly pear, have a great taste but be ready for the slippery texture.

Harvesting is the first part of taking advantage of the texture and flavor of cacti. Cacti tend to produce 20 to 40 pads every year, and while you can harvest these at any time, there are peak times for doing so to get the best flavor. Only harvest mature pads and take no more than ⅔ of a pad at a time. Remember that cactus pads have sharp spikes that can injure you. Protect yourself with thick gloves and long-sleeved clothing. Use tongs to grasp the pads. Use a sharp knife to cut the portion that you are harvesting. Wash the sliced pad and use the knife to scrape away the spines. The skin can then be peeled and the raw meat can be used as-is or cooked.

Once you have harvested your edible plants, it is time to store them for long-term use. Move to the next chapter to see how.

CHAPTER 10

STORAGE AND PRESERVATION 101

You have come in from the wild with your foraged goodies under your belt. You are feeling proud and refreshed as you should. You might be tempted to kick back, relax, and reminisce about your adventure, but wait! It is time to ensure that your goodies survive long enough for you to use during cooking. Some plants will be fresh, and some, like berries, you might want to consume right away. But for other plant parts, you will need to preserve them for long-term use. This means we need to venture into discussing topics like storing and preserving wild foods so that they last as long as possible. This chapter gives you the details you need to know.

STANDARD STORAGE PRACTICES

Storage becomes important the moment you harvest the wild plant parts. This is why breathable storage bags are a must-have for your foraging toolkit. They ensure that your goodies do not get squashed or wither during the trip to your home. Be sure to not overfill the breathable bags. As a general rule of thumb, do not use plastic to store harvested wild plants as they trap heat and moisture and lessen the shelf-life of your finds.

Harvested flowers and some greens are delicate and so are bruised easily during the process of transport. Lessen the chances of them becoming damaged by storing them between large leaves. These leaves help prevent them from losing moisture and drying out as well as help them keep their shape. In the absence of leaves, you can place them between damp towels to serve the same function.

Harvest flowers in the morning but after the sun is gracing the blooms with its rays. They are usually still closed before the sun comes up, but when the sun hits them, they are full of moisture (the best conditions for harvesting them). After the sun comes up, they start to lose that moisture and have to weather conditions like insects invading them and getting tackled by the wind.

At home, you have a few options for making sure that your foraged finds remain fresh and safe for you if you are not going to munch on them right away. The first thing you need to do is ensure that they are clean. Brush off any dust or dirt that has collected on them. Look for any stray insects and get rid of these. Refresh leaves and greens by dousing and soaking them in cold water. To do that, fill a sink with cold water and immerse the leaves. Keep them there for 10 minutes or until they perk back up if they had started to wilt. Remove the excess moisture by placing them in a salad spinner or using a towel. Air-dry the leaves and greens by placing them on a towel. Seal them in refrigerator bags with a moist paper towel and refrigerate.

Other plant parts should be cleaned as well and washed. Allow them to air dry. Depending on the specific plant part, these can be refrigerated or kept at room temperature.

PRESERVING FORAGED WILD PLANTS

Sometimes harvested wild foods just do not last very long after they have been removed from the source where they grew. However, it would be impractical to plan frequent outings just to get these items for one-time use. Also, such items may only be available for a limited window of time. So, how do you enjoy them after you have harvested them when long-term storage as-is, is not an option? The answer? Preservation.

Food preservation is the processing of food in such a way that it prevents or slows down the rate at which it spoils. It also allows you to benefit from all of the vitamins, minerals, and other nutritional content that wild plants store inside them. There are several options for preservation available to keep your wild foods for as long as possible.

Blanching and Freezing Food

This is one of the easiest methods of preserving your wild plants. Blanching is the process of cooking foods (typically fruits and veggies) by scalding them in hot water or steam for a short amount of time and then transferring them to a cold water bath to immediately stop the cooking process. Blanching stops food from losing its nutritional value, texture, color, and taste. It also removes any bacteria and dirt that might be stuck to the food.

Some wild foods require blanching while others do not. A little research on the specific wild plant you want to preserve in this way will let you know if blanching is required.

If the wild food was blanched, shake off the excess water. If it was not, rinse in cold water and shake off the excess water. Chop the wild food coarsely then place in a freezer bag or freezer-safe container and freeze. Alternatively, you can spread out the chopped pieces on a baking sheet, freeze, then transfer the frozen pieces to a

Texas Edible Wild Plant Foraging

freezer bag. Then store in the freezer.

Wild foods preserved in this way cannot be used in salads but they can be used in recipes that require cooking. They must be thawed out first. Once the wild food has been thawed, it cannot be refrozen or you risk food poisoning.

Drying

This is a traditional method of food preservation that draws out the moisture from food to prevent it from spoiling. Drying is useful because it stops the growth of yeast, bacteria, and mold so that the wild food remains safe and healthy to consume even after it would have long since gone bad otherwise. This characteristic is possible only because of the absence of moisture as it is removed during the drying process.

If you are drying flowers, remove the petals from the base if that base is thick and dry separately since the base tends to take longer to dry. Leaves and shoots can be dried as they are. Larger leaves can be cut into smaller pieces with scissors for shorter drying times. Berries can be dried as they are. Larger fruits and tubers need to be sliced thickly. Fleshier fruits and vegetables must be sprinkled with salt to draw out additional moisture and prevent the growth of bacteria.

To dry your wild foods, first, clean them by rinsing off the dirt and other debris. If the wild food is already clean, do not wet it. There are a few methods of drying available to you. The first is good, old-fashioned air drying. To do so, tie the wild food in small bundles in a breathable bag and hang the bag in a dry, airy, warm area. Do not place it in direct sunlight though or you risk causing that wild food to lose its color and flavor. You can also air dry by placing the wild food on a clean window screen or similar spread. Place in a dry, airy, warm area. Turn the wild food often to ensure it dries evenly. Depending on the particular wild food, this process can take a few

days or a few weeks.

Using a home food dehydrator or a conventional oven for drying will significantly speed up the process. To use a dehydrator, lay the wild foods out in a single layer on a tray and dry at a temperature between 40 and 50 degrees Celsius. The process will take between 4 and 6 hours normally. The process and drying time are much the same with a conventional oven.

When the foods like leaves, shoots, and flowers are dried, they will crumble easily and are crunchy to the touch. Dried fruits, veggies, and fleshier parts of wild plants tend to have a leathery, brittle texture. Store them in a mason jar with tight seals. Dried wild food has an average shelf life of up to 2 years. They can be used to increase the nutritional value of many dishes like stews and soups. I personally love placing some of my dried greens in the food processor and creating powders to infuse my smoothies, pastries, soups, and more with super nutrition.

Other ways that you can use dried wild foods include:

- To infuse vinegar and oils with more flavor
- As cake and pastry decorations
- In cocktails mixes
- To make herbal teas

Pickling

Pickling is a food preservation method that makes use of an acidic, salty solution to keep the food from going bad. An additional benefit to pickling is that it helps infuse the food with additional flavor as you can also add your favorite spices and herbs to the solution. Wild fruits and vegetables tend to be the items of choice for pickling. The items must be cleaned first. Larger items must be sliced thin before adding to the pickling solution which is called a brine.

To create a brine, combine one part water and one part distilled

vinegar in a pan. Bring this mixture to a boil, then add salt to your preference. You can also add sugar. Stir to ensure the salt and sugar are dissolved then allow the solution to cool. Transfer this solution to the sealable mason jars that you will be using to store your pickled wild food. Do not fill up to the brim. Add the wild food to the solution and ensure they are submerged. Pickled foods can be stored at room temperature or in the refrigerator. They last between 2 and 4 weeks typically.

Wild foods that I love to pickle include:

- Dandelion flower buds
- Wild onions
- Beautyberries
- Milkweed pods
- Prickly pear pads
- Queen Anne's lace roots

Jams and Jellies

Wild fruits are great for making jams and jellies. Not only do these taste great (and invite you to reminisce on happy memories from childhood) but they are also a form of food preservation. Making jams from prickly pear pads as well as blueberries is one of my favorite uses of these wild foods found in Texas. You can modify recipes to suit your particular taste but typically all that is needed is to combine the fruit (chopped if working with larger pieces like the prickly pear pads) with sugar and reduce the resulting juices that are extracted over heat. Other ingredients that can be added include:

- Pectin. This compound is typically found in higher concentrations in unripe fruits. Therefore, the amount of pectin you may need to add depends on the ripeness of the fruit that you are using. To test to see if the fruit that you are using already contains pectin, add 1 teaspoon of juice extracted from that fruit to 1 tablespoon of rubbing alcohol

and allow to stand for 2 minutes. If a solid mass forms, pectin is already naturally present in the fruit. If no mass or a weak mass forms, then you need to add pectin into the mixture.
- Acid of some sort like citrus juice or vinegar
- Fruit flavor

Once this is done, transfer the mixture to a heat-safe, sealable jar. Jams and jellies typically last for one month when stored at room temperature after you have opened them after the initial seal.

Fruit and Berry Vinegar

Fruit and berry vinegars are a great alternative to making jams and jellies with your foraged fruits. Fruit vinegars are basically fermented fruits. To make your fruit vinegar, all you need to prepare is fruit or berries, vinegar, and sugar. Combine the fruit and vinegar in a jar and smash these together. Cover the resulting mixture with the paper towels and secure it with a rubber band for between 7 and 14 days. Shake the mixture every day. Strain or stir the resulting liquid and pour it into a pan. Add sugar to suit your taste and bring this mixture to a boil before allowing it to simmer for 10 minutes. Pour the food vinegar into a mason jar and seal after it has cooled.

Fruit vinegars are a great way of infusing a burst of flavors into your salads, marinade, pickles, cocktails, and other recipes.

Oxymels

The root Greek word from which oxymel originates means acid and honey and these are the two ingredients used to make this solution. Oxymels are herbal extractions using honey and vinegar. They are a great alternative to using fruit and berry vinegar and allow you to extract flavor from a wider variety of ingredients such as twigs, leaves, roots, stems, and more parts of wild plants. I love adding a teaspoon of oxymel to my water and teas. I also sometimes use them to make salad dressings.

Texas Edible Wild Plant Foraging

A quick recipe for making oxymels includes the following ingredients to make approximately 1 cup:

- 2 cups of the wild food plant part
- ½ cup raw honey
- 1 cup apple cider vinegar

Add all the ingredients to a mason jar so that the wild plant part is completely covered. Shake them well and allow the mixture to sit for between 4 weeks and 6 months. The longer you allow the mixture to sit, the stronger the nutritional value and flavor that is pulled from the wild plant part. Shake the mixture every 3 days. Once you have completed the extraction process, strain the mixture to extract the liquid. Store the mixture in a sealable jar. Oxymels typically last for about one year.

So far in this book, we have discussed what foraging is, how you can do it ethically and sustainably, how to remain safe while doing it, the particulars on foraging in Texas, and finally, how you can store and preserve your foraged finds. Now, it is time to enter into the next part of this book – maybe the most important part, which is plant profiles for you to ID.

PART – III
Texas Wild Edible Plant Almanac

DIRECTORY 1

PLANT PROFILES AND SEASONAL CHARTS

Below you will find a listing of some of the most popular edible wild plants in Texas. Not only will I be giving details like identifying features and tips for harvesting the edible parts of these plants, but also, I will let you know where in Texas you are likely to find them. Some of these plants are only found in cultivation. As such, their population is not as abundantly found in Texas. As a result, the maps for such plants will be excluded. All of the plant details are accompanied by a full-color picture to ensure your Texan foraging adventures are as smooth sailing as possible. Scan the QR code below to get color images of the plants below.

PLANT PROFILES

Agave

Scientific Name: *Agave spp.*

Region/habitat the plant is found in:

Located in dry areas as well as landscaped spaces.

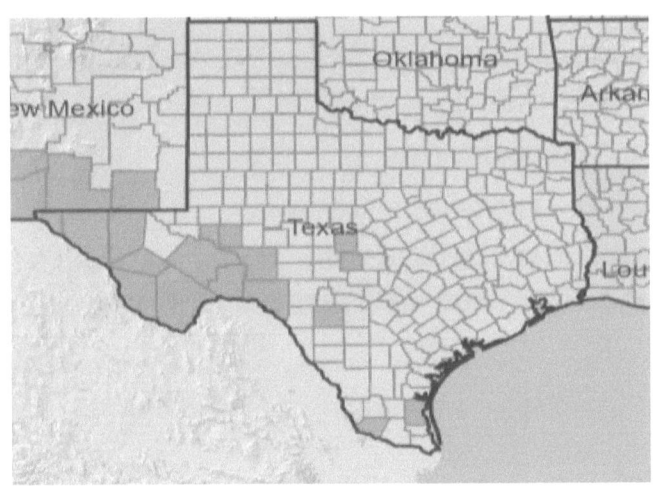

Texas Edible Wild Plant Foraging

Identifying features:

Agave comes from the succulent Asparagaceae family. They thrive in mountainous regions and dry climates, making them perfectly adapted for parts of Texas. Think of this plant as a cross between a squid and a cactus and you get the idea of what it looks like. This plant has long, sword-shaped rigid leaves with toothed edges. These leaves spread out wide. Therefore, an agave plant can span as much as 16' across.

When the plant does flower, flowers spike from the center. The flowers are funnel-shaped and brightly colored, forming in clusters. Flowers may be yellow, red, green, or white. Flower stalks can achieve a height of 10' or more

Harvesting tips:

The flowers, roots, stems, and sap of this plant can be harvested.

When harvesting this plant, ensure that the raw agave sap does not touch your skin, eyes, or any other sensitive body part. Raw agave juice can cause long-lasting burns called agave dermatitis. The affected skin turns red and blisters. This sap can cause permanent eye damage. Use protective gear such as a long-sleeved shirt, pants, gloves, a hat and sunglasses, and sharp tools when harvesting. Never eat raw agave.

Seasons for Harvesting: All year round

Preparation/Preservation tips:

- Flowers and leaves can be cooked
- Flower stocks can be roasted
- Roots and the plant body can be slow-roasted
- Sap can be fermented

Alligator Weed

Scientific Name: *Alternanthera philoxeroides*

Region/habitat the plant is found in:

Grows in spaces where full sun is received and there is shallow water

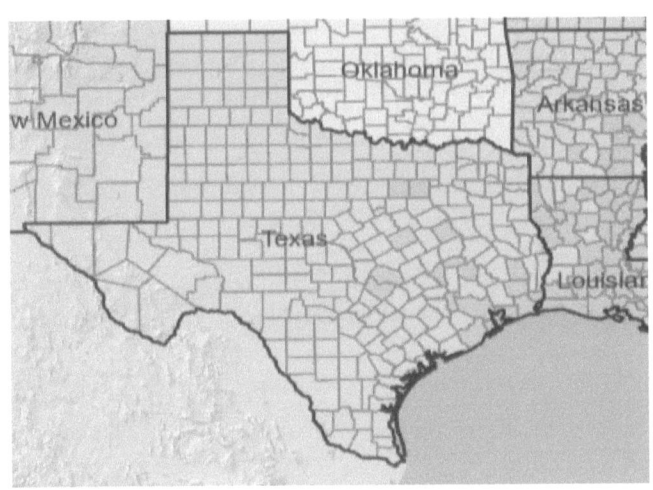

Identifying features:

This plant can be rather invasive and grows in shallow water. It is a common sight near river banks and shorelines in Texas. It is vine-like in appearance. The stems are hollow and pink and can reach up to 1m in height. The leaves are narrow and elliptical or ovate-shaped. Its flowers are white with thin petals. The flowers grow from stems that can extend away from the stem as much as 5".

Harvesting tips:

The leaves and stems of this plant can be harvested. Toxic minerals can accumulate in the soil or water where this plant grows, so ensure that you research the area before harvesting.

Seasons for Harvesting: Summer, fall, spring

Preparation/Preservation tips:

Leaves and stems can be cooked. While the leaves of this plant can be used like spinach, they should not be eaten raw. Chop the stems before cooking to minimize the toughness.

Amaranth

Scientific Name: *Amaranthus spp.*

Region/habitat the plant is found in:

Grows in sunny fields and frequently disturbed spaces.

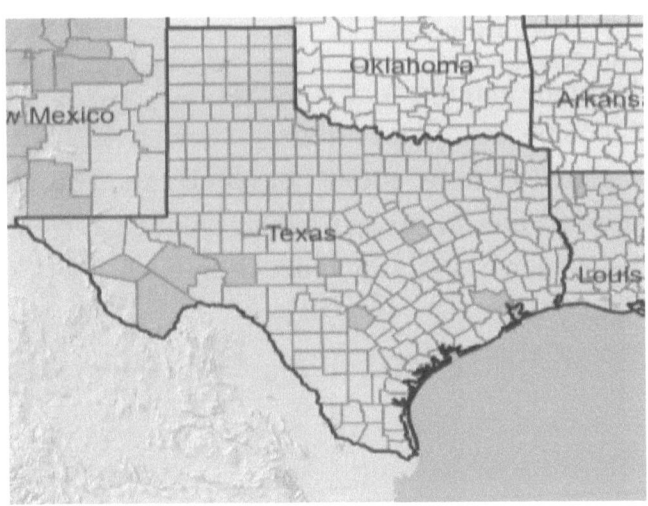

Texas Edible Wild Plant Foraging

Identifying features:

This plant's leaves are broad and egg-shaped. These leaves may be covered in tiny hairs or may be smooth depending on the exact species. The leaves may be red or green with prominent veins.

When flowering, single flowers are produced from terminal spikes. Flowers can range from red to purple. Amaranth can grow up to almost 7'.

Harvesting tips:

The seeds and leaves of this plant can be harvested.

Some species of amaranth can be harvested as soon as three months after the first shoot appears. To harvest the leaves, break off cleanly from the stem or use sharp scissors. Cut the flowers from the stem using a pair of scissors to harvest the seeds and allow them to dry in a warm, dry place. When the flowers have dried, remove the seeds by brushing them out of the flower or by beating the flowers in a bag. Use a mesh to separate the seeds from the beaten flower pieces if you use the latter method.

Seasons for Harvesting: Summer

Preparation/Preservation tips:

- Seeds can be eaten raw or roasted.
- Seeds can be ground into flour.
- Young leaves can be cooked or eaten raw. This plant is also sometimes referred to as Chinese spinach and so, its leaves can be used in a similar manner to spinach.

Bay Laurel

Scientific Name: *Persea borbonia var. borbonia*

Region/habitat the plant is found in:

Grows near Texas borders and in woodland areas.

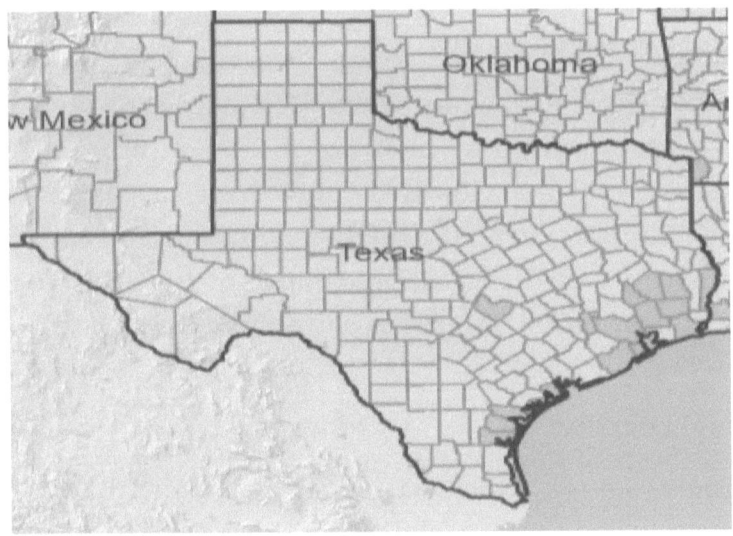

Texas Edible Wild Plant Foraging

Identifying features:

This is an evergreen tree with dense foliage. Its bark is shiny grey. The leaves have a leathery texture and are pointed and elliptical with smooth edges. They are bright green when they are young and turn darker green as they mature.

Younger bay laurel nuts are green in color and turn purple then brown as they mature. The inside of the nut (the part that is harvested) resembles an avocado pit.

Harvesting tips:

The nuts and leaves of this plant can be harvested.

Nuts can be collected from the ground after they fall off the trees. You are likely to find these with the outer flesh being brown and soft. If the outer flesh has been removed, even better, as this means less work for you during the preparation process. Never harvest moldy bay laurel nuts.

To harvest the leaves, break off cleanly from the stem or use sharp scissors.

Seasons for Harvesting: Nuts in the fall, leaves all year round

Preparation/Preservation tips:

- Nuts can be roasted or baked. Remove out of the flesh and any excess, allowing moisture to evaporate from the nuts before roasting. Roasted nuts have a flavor that is reminiscent of a mixture of dark chocolate and coffee.
- Leaves can be used as a seasoning or to make tea. To use as a seasoning, grind into a fine powder. To use as a tea, steep in boiling hot water.

Poisonous Lookalike:

- Cherry laurel, which has leaves that smell like cherry or cyanide and tooth-edged leaves, contrast with the smooth-

edged leaves and Italian seasoning smell of bay laurel.

Texas Edible Wild Plant Foraging

Bastard Cabbage

Scientific Name: *Rapistrum rugosum*

Region/habitat the plant is found in:

This plant grows in sunny fields and ditches as well as disturbed areas.

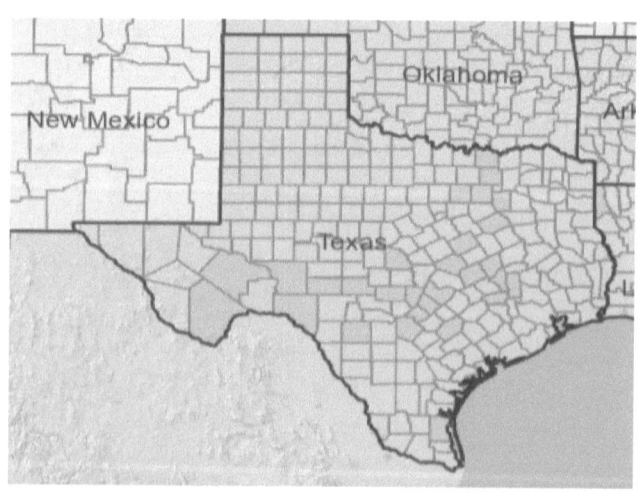

Identifying features:

This herbaceous plant typically ranges in height from 1' to 5'. It is a taproot with leaves that are wrinkled and lobed. They are typically deep green colored and can sometimes have a reddish hue. When flowering, this plant produces clusters of small yellow flowers at the tips of its multiple branches. Bastard cabbage produces a fruit called a silique. The seed capsules within are stalked and contain 1 or 2 seeds. The seeds are dark brown, smooth, small, and oval-shaped. The stems and flower buds of this plant are hairy.

Harvesting tips:

Young seed pods, flower buds, flowers, and young leaves can be harvested.

Seasons for Harvesting: Early summer, late fall, winter, spring

Preparation/Preservation tips:

- The leaves can have a slightly bitter taste but adding spices can balance this. They can be used in much the same way as spinach. Blanching the leaves first can take away the bitterness entirely.
- The flowers, seed pods, and leaves can be used to make salads or can be sauteed.
- The stems can be steamed and cooked in much the same way as you would asparagus.

Texas Edible Wild Plant Foraging

Beautyberry

Scientific Name: *Callicarpa americana and Callicarpa japonica*

Region/habitat the plant is found in:

This wild plant is found plentifully in wooded areas across Texas.

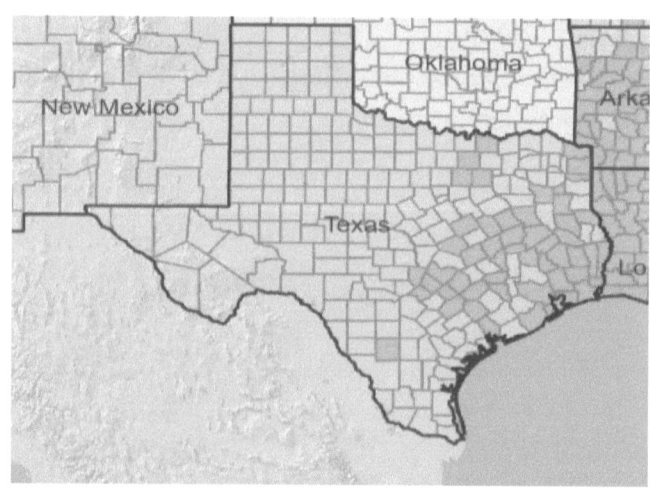

Identifying features:

Two types of beautyberries found in Texas are called the American beautyberry and the Japanese beautyberry. The difference between the two is the colors of the ripened berries vary. The American beautyberry ripens to a deep purple color while the Japanese beautyberry stays white (the color of the immature berry). Both versions of the beautyberry are edible. The beautyberries form in clusters around the branches. It is about 1 mm in size. These berries grow from clusters of pink or white flowers that appear in early summer.

The berries grow on shrubs which average between 3' to 5' but it is possible to spot them at over 9' tall if you are lucky.

Harvesting tips:

The berries of this plant are harvestable once they reach full ripeness.

Only harvest these berries if they are a deep purple color for the American version or bright white for the Japanese version. Do not harvest if they are wrinkled and dry.

Seasons for Harvesting: Late summer, fall

Preparation/Preservation tips:

- Berries can be eaten raw but be prepared for the slightly medicinal flavor. Do not eat too much of these at once at one as some people get an upset stomach from their consumption.
- Berries can be used to make jams and jellies by adding sugar and boiling before straining and pouring into sterilized jars, which should be sealed to preserve freshness.
- Berries can be used to make wines by combining with a sweeter fruit such as bananas or grapes to develop a more complex flavor and a higher alcohol index.

Texas Edible Wild Plant Foraging

Cactus - Cow's Tongue

Scientific Name: *Opuntia engelmannii var. linguiformis*

Region/habitat the plant is found in:

This plant is not commonly found but when it is, it is typically located in landscaped areas and sunny fields.

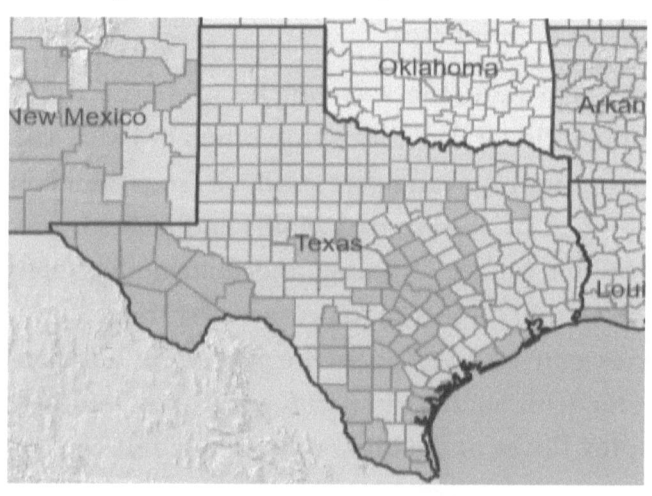

Identifying features:

These succulents can grow up to an average of 10' with wide branches that produce long, narrow pads that look like their namesake - a cow's tongue. This plant produces bright yellow flowers in the spring. These blooms give way to purple-red fruit in the summertime. As beautiful as these are, you have to beware of the sharp needles called glochids. They are found along the length of the pads and fruit.

Harvesting tips:

The fruit, pads, and flowers of this plant can be harvested.

The glochids pose a scratch and burn risk so you need to be careful when harvesting the parts of this plant. Use protective wear as well as tongs to harvest the fruit and pads.

Seasons for Harvesting: Pads all year round, fruit in the fall, flowers in the spring

Preparation/Preservation tips:

- Pads can be peeled and cooked as you would green beans. Simply be aware that these will have a slimier feel. The peeled pads can also be sprinkled with jerk spices and then dehydrated to create a vegan jerky. Alternatively, the pads can be fried.
- Juices can be made by peeling, mashing, boiling, and then straining the fruit. Simply add ice or chill and enjoy. The fruit has a naturally sweet flavor so no sweetener is needed.
- Before using the pads or fruit, you need to remove the glochids. Do so by burning them off with a torch or on a stovetop.
- Jellies, ice cream, and wines can be made from the juice of the fruit.
- The juice can be reduced to create a syrup.

Texas Edible Wild Plant Foraging

- The fruit can be eaten raw or blended to create a smoothie.
- Flowers can be eaten raw.

Cactus – Prickly Pear

Scientific Name: *Opunita lindheimeri*

Region/habitat the plant is found in:

These are more plentiful than cow's tongue and are typically located in sunny fields.

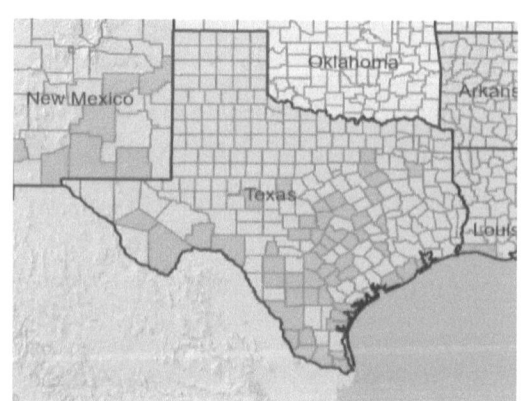

Identifying features:

This cactus is closely related to cow's tongue and so they share many physical characteristics. Just like the cow's tongue, it has flattened, leafless stems that are divided into segments called pads. The fruit is pear-shaped (hence the name of the wild plant) and varies in color between yellow, green, orange, purple, and red. It produces bright yellow flowers in early summer. The succulent has tough skin and prickles along its surface.

Harvesting tips:

The pads, fruit, flowers, and seeds of this plant can be harvested. The same times that applied to the cow's tongue for the harvesting of the pads, fruits, and flowers also apply to the prickly pear. Be sure to wear protective gear since the prickles are sharp and cause painful abrasions when they come into contact with bare skin.

The seeds are a product of the ripened fruit. Remove the seeds from the fruit's pulp and wash with clean water. Dry them in a paper towel for 1 to 2 weeks.

Seasons for Harvesting: Pads all year round, fruit in the late summer, flowers in the spring, seeds in the late summer

Preparation/Preservation tips:

- The same preparation tips that applied to the cow's tongue apply to this cactus as well.
- The seeds can be roasted or eaten raw.

Texas Edible Wild Plant Foraging

Canna Lily

Scientific Name: *Canna indica*

Region/habitat the plant is found in:

This plant is typically found in landscaped areas and sunny spots. It is a common sight.

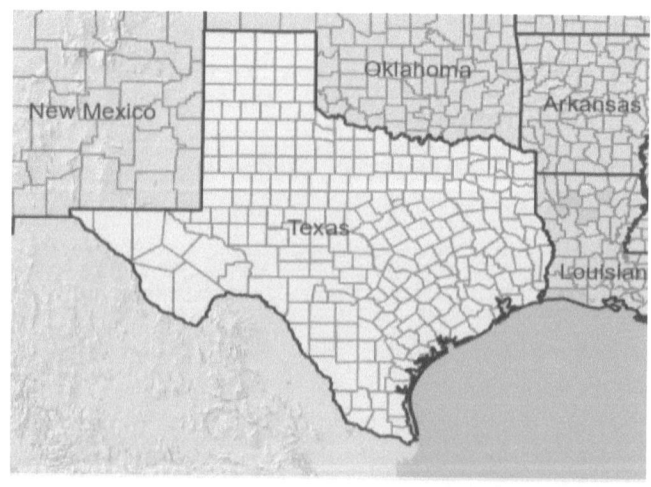

Identifying features:

One of the most distinguishing features of this plant is its leaves, which can be used to wrap foods that are being boiled or roasted. This is a handy tip if you find yourself roughing it in the wild or you want to add a little panache to your cooking style at home. The leaf can range in color from bright green to maroon. The plant produces big, bright flowers that resemble irises. They can be yellow, red, or orange. The bold hues add a dramatic effect to any scene.

The plant normally grows to a height of about 2.5'.

Harvesting tips:

The young shoots and tubers (roots) of this plant can be harvested.

Harvest the tubers by slicing from the stem. Simply gently pull up the young shoots for harvesting.

Seasons for Harvesting: Summer, fall

Preparation/Preservation tips:

- The tubers can be cooked like you would potatoes. They can be eaten raw but cooking makes them more edible and tastier.
- The tubers can also be used to make flour. Slice the tubers into ¼" rings and allow them to dry for 2 days. Crumble in water to obtain the starch that will be ground into flour.
- The tubers can be used to make alcohol.
- The shoots can be cooked like you would asparagus.

Texas Edible Wild Plant Foraging

Dayflower

Scientific Name: *Commelina communis*

Region/habitat the plant is found in:

This plant is found in quite a few areas in Texas such as landscaped areas, shared and partial sunny spots, fields, and wooded areas.

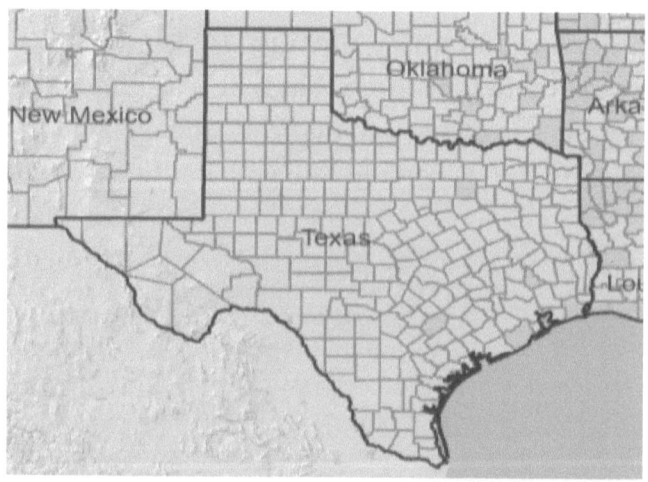

Identifying features:

This plant gets its name from the fact that its bright blue flowers appear in the morning but disappear by afternoon, becoming shriveled up after midday. The stems of the plant are weak and so the plant would creep if there were not so many stems crowding the area to force the plant body upright.

The leaves are bright green with pointed tips and a parallel vein.

Harvesting tips:

The stems, leaves, and flowers of the dayflower can be harvested. Use the usual harvesting tips outlined previously to gather these parts of the plant.

Seasons for Harvesting: Spring, late summer, fall

Preparation/Preservation tips:

- The stems can be boiled, used in soups, and steamed like spinach.
- The leaves can be used to make salads, eaten raw, or cooked.
- The flowers can be eaten raw or cooked.

Texas Edible Wild Plant Foraging

Duckweed

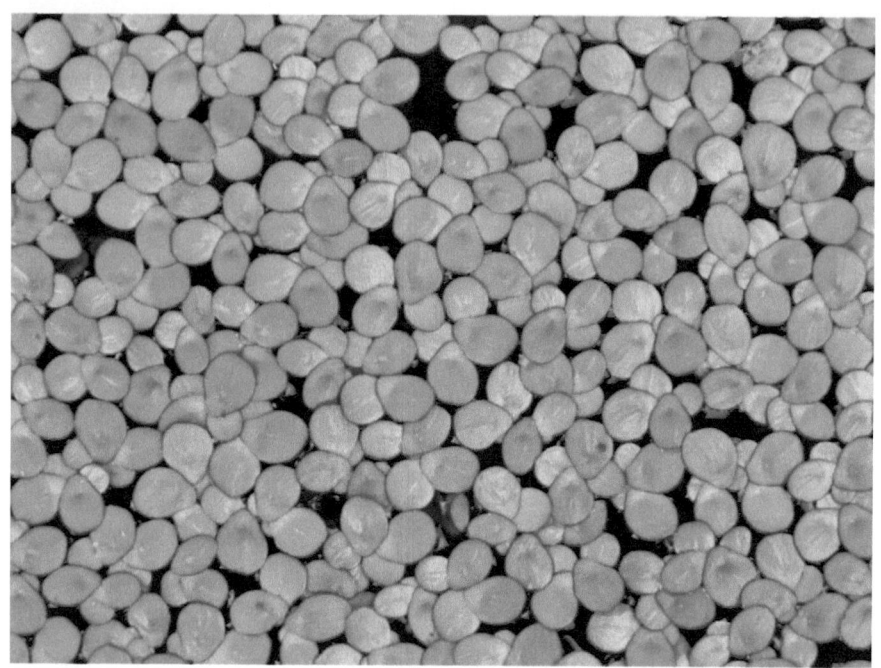

Scientific Name: *Spirodela polyrhiza and Lemna minor*

Region/habitat the plant is found in:

This plant is found plentifully in sunny areas with open water.

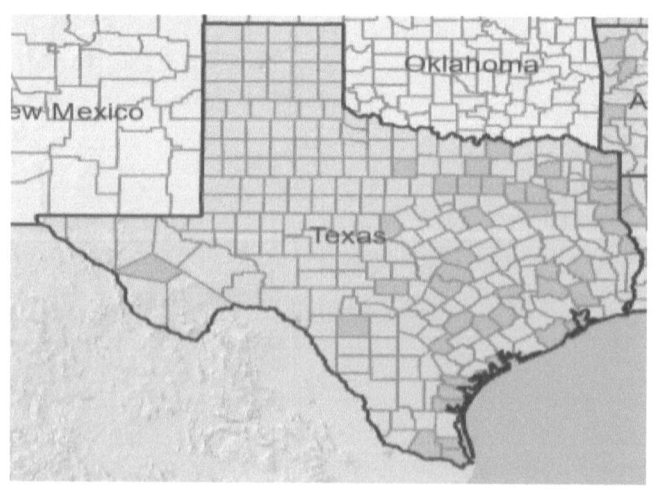

Identifying features:

These plants are fast-producing and can completely cover a still or slow-moving water surface in a little over one day. The individual aquatic plants are small with egg-shaped, flat leaves. The leaf is no more than ¼" in size.

These plants have adventitious roots that allow them to stabilize themselves on the water's surface.

Harvesting tips:

The entire plant is harvestable. To harvest, rake the leaves together along the water's face then simply collect.

Seasons for Harvesting: Summer

Preparation/Preservation tips:

- The plant must be cooked to kill any bacteria that might have accumulated along its length. Do not eat raw.
- Can be pureed to add as a thickening agent to stews and soups.
- Can be sauteed.
- Can be dried then powdered and added to food to add a nutritional kick since it is high in protein and also contains fat and fiber.

Texas Edible Wild Plant Foraging

Farkleberry

Scientific Name: *Vaccinium arboreum*

Region/habitat the plant is found in:

Farkleberry is not a common sight in Texas but it can sometimes be found in wooded areas.

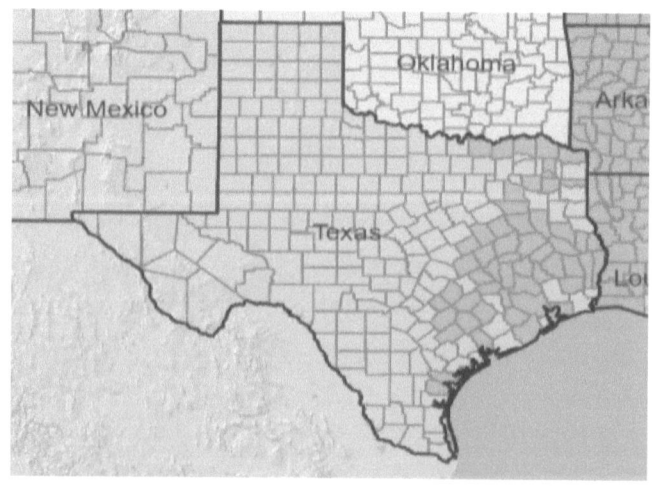

Identifying features:

The plant produces small white flowers that are bell-shaped and highly fragrant. Its leaves are elliptical and have a glossy green hue. The unripened berries, typically found mid-summer, are green. The ripe berries are black and contain tiny seeds. They are only a few millimeters big. These berries are still edible after they take on a raisin-like appearance after drying up.

The tree regularly reaches a height of approximately 15' but don't be surprised if you encounter one as tall as 25'. The tree normally has an irregular shape with crooked branches.

Harvesting tips:

The berries of this small tree can be harvested. Gently break off the berry from the main stem.

Seasons for Harvesting: Fall, winter

Preparation/Preservation tips:

- Berries can be eaten raw and are full of antioxidants.
- Berries can be cooked and reduced to make jams and jellies.
- Can also be used to make wine.

Frog Fruit

Scientific Name: *Lippia nodiflora*

Region/habitat the plant is found in:

This plant is a common sight in sunny fields, landscaped areas, and even in neighborhood yards.

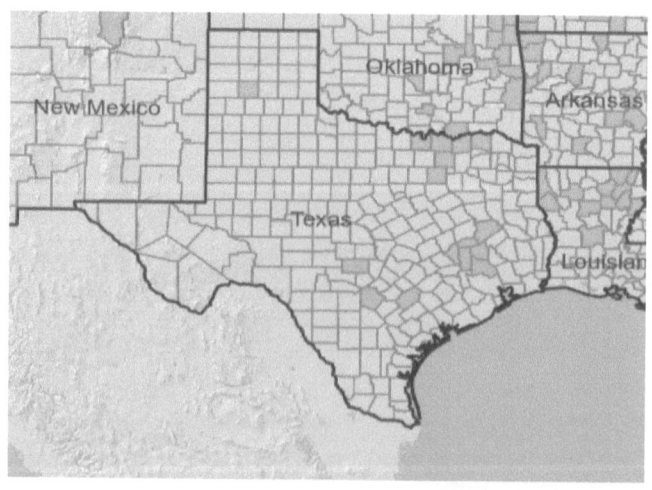

Identifying features:

Despite the name, frog fruit does not have a fruit that resembles a frog. In fact, the plant doesn't even produce fruit. The plant grows to about 5" and produces distinguishable flowers between May and October. It contains 5 petals and is white. The flowers congregate in clusters that look like pineapples. Its leaves are small with notches along the edges and they have a pinnate vein arrangement.

Harvesting tips:

The leaves are harvestable and should be cut with scissors or gently plucked from the stem.

Seasons for Harvesting: Spring, summer

Preparation/Preservation tips:

- Can be eaten raw but the texture and taste do not suit many palates.
- Can be steeped to make tea.
- Can be cooked or smoked.

Texas Edible Wild Plant Foraging

Ginkgo

Scientific Name: *Ginkgo biloba*

Region/habitat the plant is found in:

This plant is rarely found but when it is, it is normally in a wooded or landscaped space.

Identifying features:

This tree averages a height of 100' with a stem that is 8' in diameter. The bark of the stem is normally gray-tinged with a rough texture. The leaves of ginkgo are fan-shaped and divided into two lobes that are connected by a central notch. They grow to about 3" wide. The leathery-textured leaves change from dull green to yellow-green in summer, then yellow in fall before falling off the tree in late fall.

Male and female trees are separate. Pollination occurs when pollen grains are carried by the wind from male to female trees. When this happens, the female trees produce paired fruits that turn from green to yellow seeds that resemble plums. Inside of this is a nut surrounded by pulp.

Harvesting tips:

The leaves and nuts of this plant can be harvested. Harvest the leaves as normal. The nuts (or seeds) are found on the inside of the ripened fruits. The fruit of this plant smells terrible (like butter gone bad) and contains harmful chemicals. Do not eat this. Also, do not let the raw pulp of this fruit touch your mouth, eyes, and skin. To harvest the nuts, wear rubber gloves to remove the pulp from around the nut. Wash the nuts thoroughly to remove any residue.

Seasons for Harvesting: Nuts in summer, leaves in spring, summer, and fall

Preparation/Preservation tips:

- Leaves can be eaten raw and steeped to make tea.
- The nuts should be roasted since eating the raw nuts can cause an upset stomach.

Texas Edible Wild Plant Foraging

Ground Cherry

Scientific Name: *Physalis species*

Region/habitat the plant is found in:

Sighting this plant is not common but it can be found in fields and wooded areas.

Identifying features:

This is a vine-like plant that grows to about 1' tall. Its leaves are velvety and look similar to that of tomatillos with pointed edges.

The fruit is wrapped in a husk that has a parchment-like feeling. Ripe, the fruit is yellow or orange with yellow seeds. They taste like a cross between a tomato and a pineapple.

Harvesting tips:

The fruits of this plant can be harvested. Be sure to only use ripe versions as eating the unripe fruits can cause vomiting, diarrhea, and upset stomach. The seeds of the ground cherry are also edible and add a crunchy texture to the palate. The fruits usually drop to the ground before they are ripe so all you have to do to harvest is pick the fruit off the ground and store them in an open container. Wait until the fruit ripens before use.

Seasons for Harvesting: Summer, fall

Preparation/Preservation tips:

- Fruits can be eaten raw or cooked just like you would tomatillos. Simply remove the outer husk before use.
- Fruits can also be dried to create "raisins."

Texas Edible Wild Plant Foraging

Honey Locust

Scientific Name: *Gleditsia Triacanthos*

Region/habitat the plant is found in:

This plant is found plentifully in sunny dry areas where it rains little.

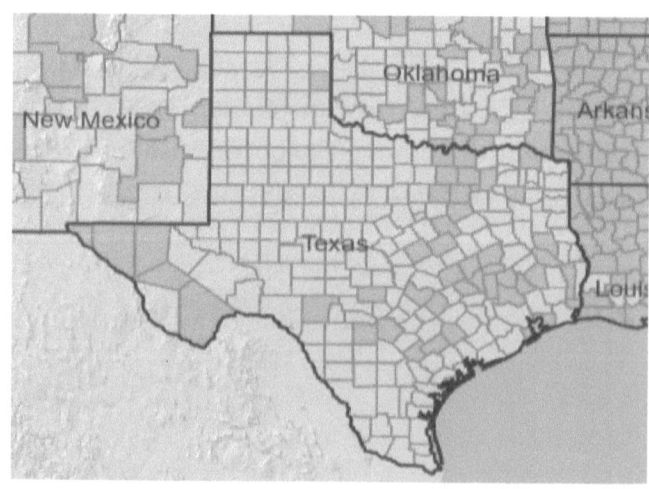

Identifying features:

This is a spiky tree from the pea family and typically grows up to a height of 130'. Thorns appear along the length of the stem and branches. It bears compound leaves with several leaflets. The flowers which appear in clusters tend to also be green and blend into the foliage. However, they sometimes appear slightly white. The fruits of this plant are oval-shaped, flattened, and elongated. They are called pods. They can appear twisted and grow about 18" long. The flesh is sweet and surrounds bean-like seeds. The matured pods turn from green to brown.

The plant gets its name from the yellow sap between the seeds of the pods. It tastes like honey whether the pod is young or mature.

Harvesting tips:

The seeds, flowers, pods, and buds of this plant can be harvested.

Young pods can be picked from the tree while dropped mature pods can be picked off the ground. The other edible parts of the plant can be harvested as normal.

Seasons for Harvesting: Spring, summer

Preparation/Preservation tips:

- Buds and flowers can be steeped to create tea.
- Each part is edible raw but great when cooked in soups and stews.
- Young pods can be cooked like you would green beans.
- Mature pods can be ground into flour. Remove the outer casing to create.

Texas Edible Wild Plant Foraging

Indian Strawberry

Scientific Name: *Duchesnea indica*

Region/habitat the plant is found in:

This plant is typically found in partially shaded or sunny fields and moist areas.

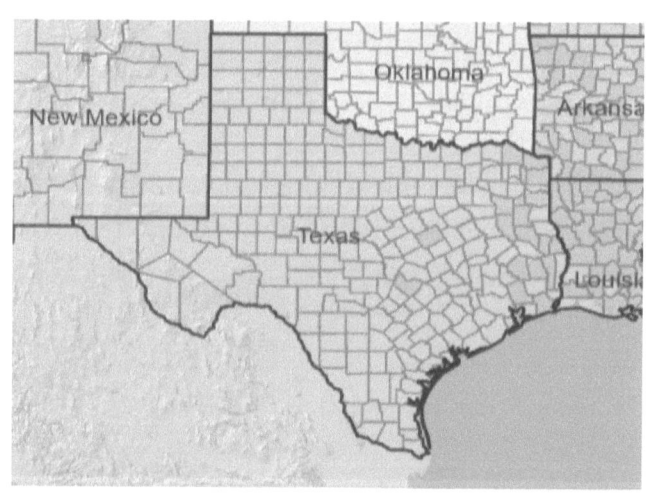

Identifying features:

Also called mock strawberry, this plant is a runner. The stem grows to about 1' but the plant typically only achieves a height of 2.5".

It produces attractive yellow flowers that rise out of the stem's joints. Each flower has 5 petals and blooms between April and June. The leaves are toothed along the edges. They along with the stems are hairy.

The plant gets its name because the fruit resembles small strawberries. They do not have the flavor or juiciness of strawberries.

Harvesting tips:

The fruit, young leaves, and flowers of this plant can be harvest as described earlier in this book.

Seasons for Harvesting: Spring

Preparation/Preservation tips:

- All edible parts of this plant can be eaten raw. However, the fruit tends to taste bland.
- Leaves and flowers can be steeped to make tea.
- All edible parts can be cooked.

Japanese Hawkweed

Scientific Name: *Crepis japonica and Youngia japonica*

Region/habitat the plant is found in:

This plant is not hard to find especially along disturbed areas.

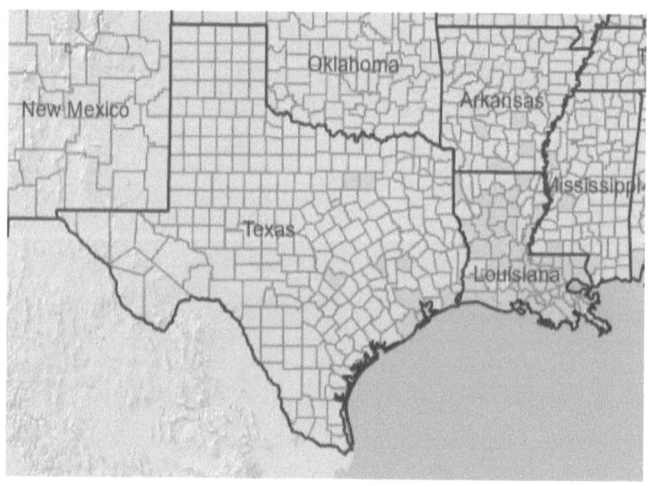

Identifying features:

These plants are small, only achieving a width of 12" while growing to about twice that height. These plants are grass-like and grow in clusters. A close relative of dandelions, the two plants are often mistaken. However, the difference is that the Japanese hawkweed has small clusters of small yellow flowers that are too small to be used like those of dandelions.

Harvesting tips:

The young shoots, young roots, and young leaves of this plant can be harvest as described earlier in this book.

Seasons for Harvesting: Spring, fall, winter

Preparation/Preservation tips:

- All edible parts of the plant can be eaten raw or cooked.
- The leaves are slightly bitter. Boil and add your favorite seasonings and spices to elevate the flavor. They can also be used in salads.
- Roots can be roasted to make coffee.

Kudzu

Scientific Name: *Pueraria species - P. lobata, P. montana, P. edulis, P. phaseoloides and P. thomsoni*

Region/habitat the plant is found in:

This is an invasive plant that is found plentifully in fields, farms, and yards.

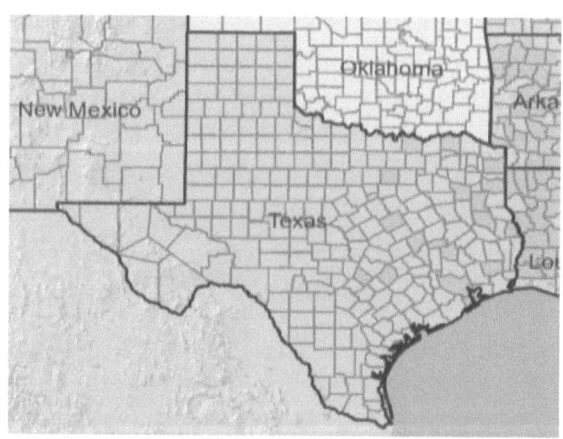

Identifying features:

This plant resembles poison ivy but it's far less toxic than it lookalike. This climbing vine produces compound leaflets that are about 4" across. The leaflets have hairy margins and are deeply lobed. The plant produces individual flowers that are purple and hang in clusters. The flowers appear in the late summer and they produce hairy, brown seed pods that typically contain between 3 and 10 hard seeds.

These plants are highly invasive and tend to kill other plants so be careful not to transplant this wild plant to your yard.

Harvesting tips:

The vine tips, flowers, roots, and young leaves of this plant can be harvested as usual.

Seasons for Harvesting: All year round

Preparation/Preservation tips:

- Flowers can be eaten raw or steeped to make tea.
- The leaves and vine tips can be cooked. Simply add your favorite seasonings and spices for a unique flavor.
- Roots can be scraped to get to the starch.

Poisonous Lookalike:

Poison ivy. They have similar leaves that are compound with three broad large leaflets.

Texas Edible Wild Plant Foraging

Lady's Thumb

Scientific Name: *Polygonum persicaria*

Willow Walsh

Region/habitat the plant is found in:

This plant is found in moist, sunny spots typically along water body banks.

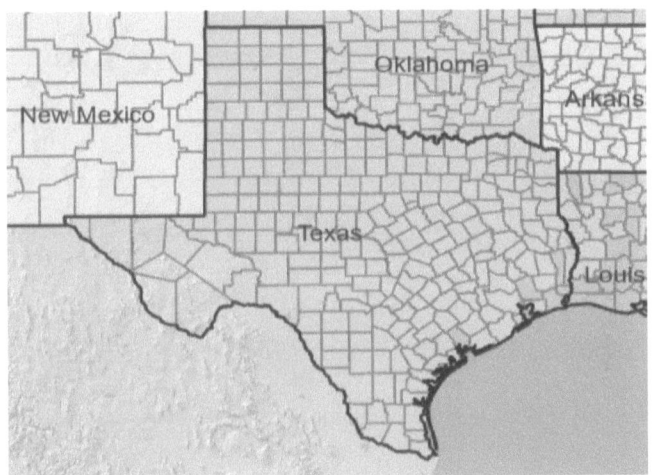

Identifying features:

Lady's thumb normally grows to a height of about 24". This small plant gets its name from the dark mark in the center of its leaves that looks like a lady's thumbprint. These leaves are typically between 3" and 4" long and have a pointed tip. Another notable feature of this wild plant is its flowers, which hang in a dense cluster along a green stem. They are spike-like in appearance and either pink or purple.

Harvesting tips:

The leaves of this plant can be harvested and must be cooked to be consumed. Simply gently tug them free or snip with scissors.

Seasons for Harvesting: Spring, summer

Preparation/Preservation tips:

- It is best to cook the leaves of the plant before eating to ensure any bacteria is killed. Can be boiled, sauteed, or added to stews and soups.

Texas Edible Wild Plant Foraging

Lizard's Tail

Scientific Name: *Saururus cernuus*

Region/habitat the plant is found in:

This plant is not a common find but it can be located in moist areas such as along the edges of water bodies.

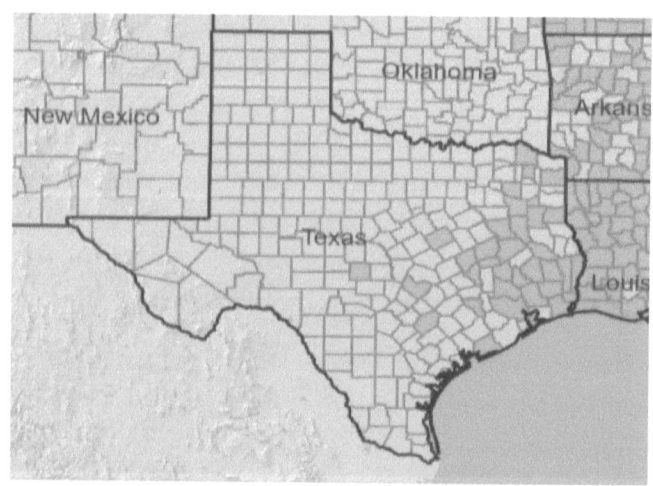

Identifying features:

This plant gets its name from the spike of white flowers that it produces. The bunch looks like a lizard's tail as it droops at the end. The typical length is 6" to 8" but it can grow longer. These tails normally appear in April to blossom in May. There is normally no sign of them by July. These flower clusters grow opposite a leaf. The leaves are triangular with a cordate base. The plant grows upright and normally reaches a height of 4'.

Harvesting tips:

The leaves and roots of this plant can be harvested.

Seasons for Harvesting: Spring, summer, fall

Preparation/Preservation tips:

- Because these edible parts have no nutritional value, they are typically used to make medicinal teas. To do this, steep the leaves in hot water or boil the sliced roots.

Magnolia

Scientific Name: *Magnolia grandiflora*

Region/habitat the plant is found in:

Commonly found in woods and landscaped areas.

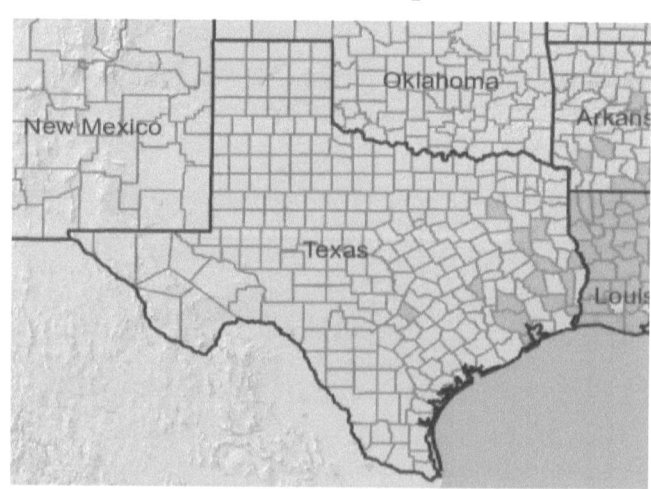

Identifying features:

This tree grows up to 120' tall and has a single stem. The leaves of this evergreen plant have green tops and brown undersides. These elliptical leaves grow in an alternating pattern and tend to be between 5" and 10" in length. They are between 2" and 5" in width, having a thick and leathery texture.

This plant has distinguishable white flowers that bloom like a bowl and open into a spectacular display of 6 to 12 petals. As they mature, the petals turn brown. When this happens, the magnolia flower gives way to a fuzzy seed head (fruit). This seedhead bursts open in the fall to reveal the hard, red seeds inside.

Harvesting tips:

The leaves and flowers of this plant can be harvested. The best time to harvest magnolia flowers is just when they are beginning to open. They turn brown quickly after opening and should not be harvested then.

It should be noted that you might see the seeds listed as edible in some sources while others list them as poisonous. To be on the safe side, I would stay away from them.

Seasons for Harvesting: Leaves all year round, flowers in spring

Preparation/Preservation tips:

- Leaves and flowers can be steeped to make tea.
- Flowers can be pickled.

Milkweed

Scientific Name: *Asclepias spp.*

Region/habitat the plant is found in:

This plant can be spotted sporadically in fields around Texas.

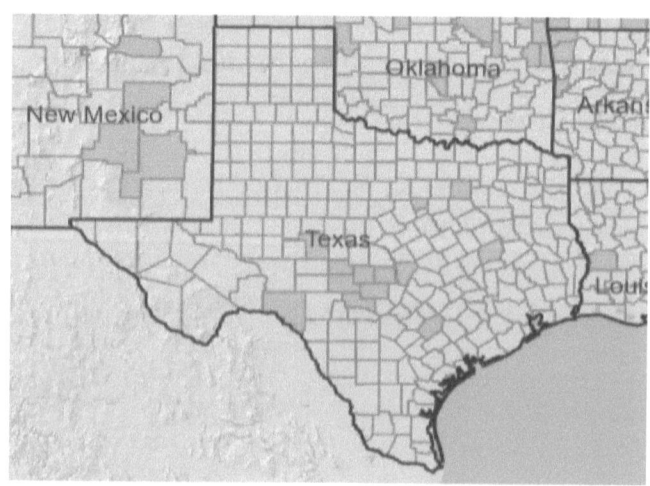

Identifying features:

Several species of butterfly such as monarchs and milkweed butterflies rely on milkweed plants (which grow to about 6' tall) exclusively as a food source to feed their larvae. This is because the plant contains a milky juice that makes the larvae and their subsequent growth stages distasteful to predators.

This milky substance is derived from the flowers of this plant. This sap can be seen when the plant is broken. The flowers are hairy and have five united petals occuring in clusters. The color of these flowers ranges from a variety of pink shades to white or even purple.

The plant produces pod-like fruits and silky-haired seeds. These seeds are flat, reddish-brown, and about ¼" long.

Harvesting tips:

The young flower buds, fruits, and shoots of this plant are edible. Harvest as you normally would.

Seasons for Harvesting: Spring, summer

Preparation/Preservation tips:

- All edible parts of this part can be cooked or eaten raw.
- Boil the edible parts to remove any bitter taste. Change the water as needed to get rid of this bitter taste completely.

Poisonous Lookalike:

Dogbane is a similar-looking plant but it is smaller. The white, milky sap that dogbane produces blisters skin. Another difference between the two plants is that milkweed has white hairs on its stem.

Texas Edible Wild Plant Foraging

Nasturtium

Scientific Name: *Tropaeolum majus*

Region/habitat the plant is found in:

This plant can be found infrequently in flower beds and yards.

Identifying features:

Also known as Indian cress, nasturtium are plants that can be found as compact bushes or creeping like vines depending on the exact environment. They grow to about 12' tall. Their leaves are round and their flowers make a bold statement with bright red, orange, or yellow hues. The flowers are funnel-shaped and contain a sweet nectar.

This plant contains characteristics that drive away insects that will nibble away on plants such as cucumbers, tomatoes, and fruit trees. Therefore, they are a good addition to any garden.

Harvesting tips:

The flowers and leaves of this plant are edible. Harvest as you normally would.

Seasons for Harvesting: Spring, summer

Preparation/Preservation tips:

- Flowers and leaves can be eaten raw. They have a spicy, peppery-radish taste and can be used to elevate the taste of salads or added to condiments like mayonnaise for a spicy kick.
- Flowers can also be added to pickled foods for extra flavor.

Ocotillo

Scientific Name: *Fouquieria splendens*

Region/habitat the plant is found in:

This plant is a common find on hillsides, sunny areas, and dry spots.

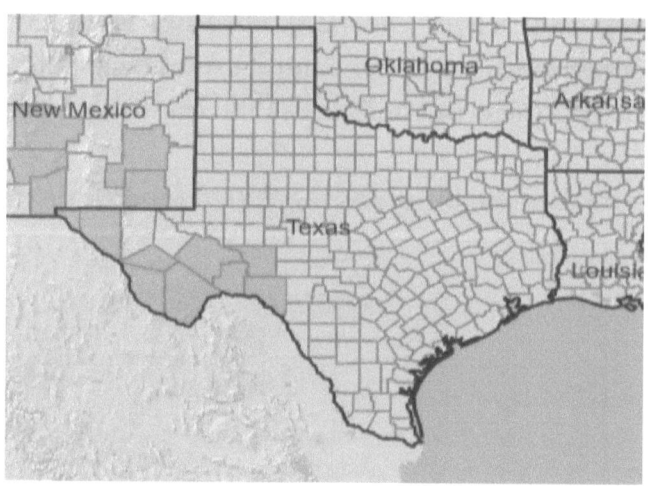

Identifying features:

This plant is often mistaken for a leafless, thorny cactus as it spends most of the year without leaves and is tall, growing up to 20'. However, after a good dose of rain, leaves sprout. These leaves are small and round and will soon be gone once the rainfall is.

This plant produces clusters of red tubular flowers that bloom late in the winter through to spring. Once these flowers drop, the seeds will appear and soon be ready to harvest.

Harvesting tips:

The flowers and seeds of this plant are edible.

Seasons for Harvesting: Flowers from late winter to spring, seeds from spring to early summer

Preparation/Preservation tips:

- The flowers on this plant can be dried and used to make tea.
- Seeds can be ground to create flour or pounded into a powder to create a porridge.

Texas Edible Wild Plant Foraging

Onion - Wild

Scientific Name: *Allium species*

Region/habitat the plant is found in:

These plants are found plentifully in sunny, open areas across Texas.

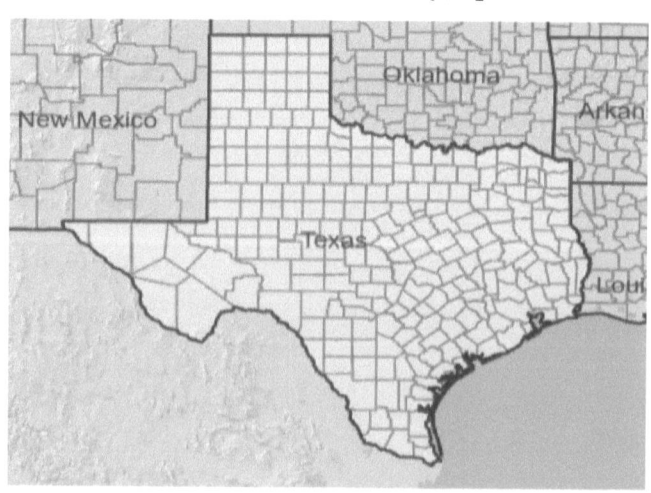

Identifying features:

This plant typically grows to a height of between 12" to 14". An individual wild onion resembles a green onion. These plans typically grow in large beds. It produces small white flowers that eventually turn into hard seeds. The flowers are umbels with six petals.

The scent of the plant is reminiscent of onion or garlic.

Harvesting tips:

The leaves, young stems, flowers, and bulbs of this plant are edible. Gently pull up the plant to expose the bulbs and harvest the rest of the plants as usual.

Seasons for Harvesting: All year round

Preparation/Preservation tips:

- All edible parts of this plant can be eaten raw or cooked.
- Flowers can be eaten raw and add an interesting appearance to salads.
- Bigger wild onions are typically tougher to eat raw and should be cooked. They can be boiled or stewed. You can determine the toughness of the wild onion by noting how easy it is to break during harvesting.

Poisonous Lookalike:

Rain lilies (*Zephyranthes stellaris*) look like wild onions. Consuming them can lead to death.

Crows Poison (*Nothoscordum bivalve*) also looks like wild onion. Eating the parts of this plant can cause an upset stomach.

The noticeable difference between these two plants and wild onion is that wild onion smells like an onion while the others smell like grass.

Passion Vine

Scientific Name: *Passiflora incarnata*

Region/habitat the plant is found in:

These plants are a common sight in sunny fields, yards, and along borders across Texas.

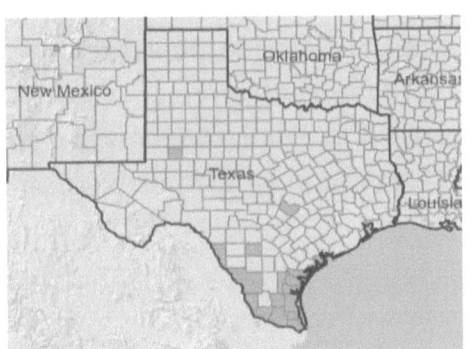

Texas Edible Wild Plant Foraging

Identifying features:

Also called maypop (because of the sound that they make when they are burst open), these plants have three-lobed leaves. The vines can climb up to 30' high as the plant clings to stronger plants and trees. The plant produces pink and white flowers that are approximately 3" across. The shallow flowers are saucer-shaped and feature 5 petals, 5 sepals and many thread-like tendrils.

This plant's fruits are green initially but turn into yellow or purple berries that look like orbs. Inside is a yellow juice and small dark seeds.

Harvesting tips:

The ripe fruits, flowers, and leaves of this plant can be edible. The ripe fruits are ready to harvest when the yellow version is almost golden and the purple version looks almost black, and when they fall off the vine. The fruit will appear slightly wrinkled when it is ready to harvest.

The flowers do not last very long and should be harvested as soon as they bloom.

Harvest these parts as you normally would.

Seasons for Harvesting: Late summer, fall, early winter

Preparation/Preservation tips:

- Fruits can be used to make juice by slicing them open, extracting the pulp, and adding them to water. Strain to remove the seeds and add sweetener as desired.
- Fruits can be used to make preserves and jams.
- Leaves and flowers can be used to make preserves and jams.

Pimpernel

Scientific Name: *Anagallis arvensis*

Region/habitat the plant is found in:

This plant is a common sight in sunny fields and yards in Texas.

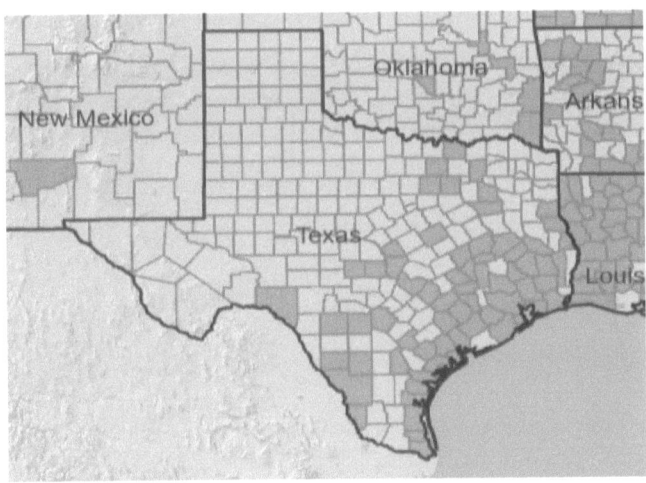

Texas Edible Wild Plant Foraging

Identifying features:

This wildflower, which typically grows to a height of about 1', is characterized by square stems. Its leaves are oval and grow opposite each other. Pimpernel flowers can be blue, orange, red, or white and are star-shaped. These flowers only achieve a size of about ¼" across and close up just before it rains. This second feature makes this plant a great tool for predicting when bad weather is approaching. The flowers also close up at dusk and only reopen when touched by sunlight.

Harvesting tips:

The leaves, flowers, and stems of this plant are edible. Harvest as usual.

Seasons for Harvesting: Spring, summer

Preparation/Preservation tips:

- All of the edible parts of this plant can be dried and then powered to produce tea.
- Young leaves can be eaten raw or cooked but tend to be too bitter to be enjoyable.

Pineapple Weed

Scientific Name: *Matricaria discoidea*

Region/habitat the plant is found in:

This plant is not a common find but it can be spotted in areas where there is disturbed soil like along dirt roads and driveways.

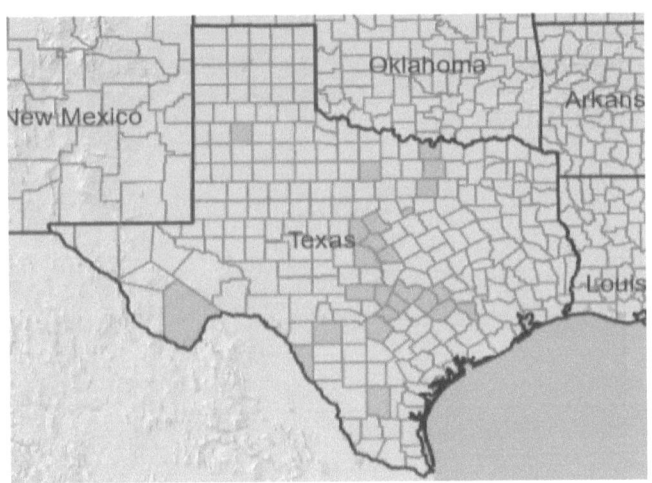

Texas Edible Wild Plant Foraging

Identifying features:

This is a short plant that has an average height of 16". Its stems are short, lined with many branches that come from a base. The leaves are alternate and fern-like. The flowers are yellow, cone-shaped, and produce a light brown fruit that has a single seed. Like the namesake, the pineapple weed flowers taste like pineapples. The crushed leaves and flowers smell like pineapples, as well.

Harvesting tips:

The flowers and leaves of this plant are edible. Harvest as you normally would.

Seasons for Harvesting: Spring, summer, fall

Preparation/Preservation tips:

- The flowers and leaves can be eaten raw or dried to make tea. The tea is calming like chamomile tea.

Queen Anne's Lace

Scientific Name: *Daucus Carot and Daucus Pusillus*

Region/habitat the plant is found in:

This plant is an infrequent site around the fields in Texas.

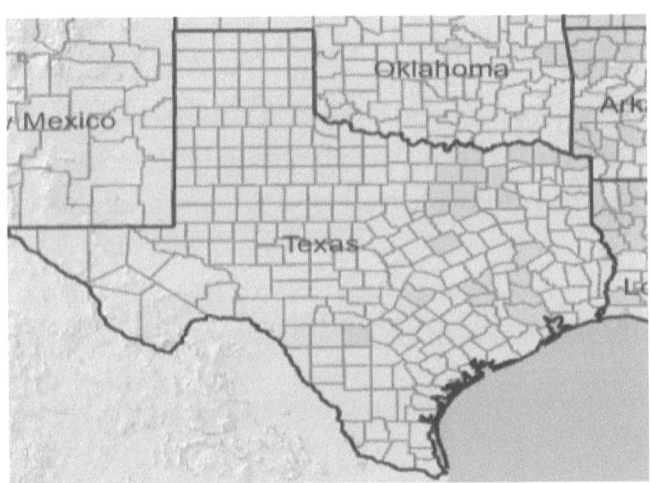

Identifying features:

Also called wild carrot, this plant grows to about 5' tall and is easily identified by the cluster of small white flowers that it produces. These flowers are umbel-shaped and can have a solitary purple or red flower in the center, blooming in late spring up until mid-fall.

Its leaves are small and fern-like. The leaves and stems produce a carrot-like odor when crushed. The stem is hairy with red stripes.

Harvesting tips:

The young shoots, young roots, flowers, flower stems, and seeds of this plant are edible. Harvest these as you normally would.

Seasons for Harvesting: Early summer

Preparation/Preservation tips:

- Shoots and roots that are harvested in the first year can be eaten raw or cooked. They make a great addition to stews and soups.

Texas Edible Wild Plant Foraging

- Flower stems that are harvested in the second year can be eaten raw or cooked.
- Flowers can be made into jelly.
- Seeds can serve as a spicy substitute for celery seeds.

Poisonous Lookalike:

Water hemlock is a poisonous Queen Anne's Lace lookalike. The differences between these two plants include Queen Anne's Lace produces a tiny red or purple flower in the center of the white flower cluster, Queen Anne's Lace's roots smell like carrots and water hemlock has a very terrible scent. Water hemlock also has a white powder on its stems and this is absent from Queen Anne's Lace.

Redbud

Scientific Name: *Cercis canadensis*

Region/habitat the plant is found in:

These are found plentifully in landscaped and wooded areas.

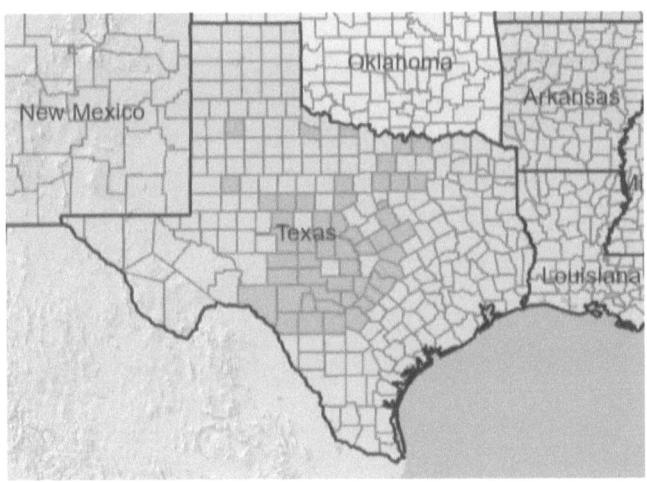

Texas Edible Wild Plant Foraging

Identifying features:

This tree grows to about 30' and is highly picturesque with a purple-colored trunk and pink flowers that appear in clusters along the branches and stems. Its leaves are heart-shaped and are arranged in an alternate pattern. These produce a red-brown fruit that is approximately 4" long and produces purple seeds that turn brown when dried out.

Harvesting tips:

The seed pods and flowers of this plant can be harvested to eat. The opened flowers are sweeter than those that are still closed so it is better to harvest those. Harvest the seeds while they are still purple as they become tough and slightly bitter as they mature.

Seasons for Harvesting: Flowers in spring, seeds after flowers have matured

Preparation/Preservation tips:

- The flowers are sweet and can be eaten raw or cooked.
- Seeds can be eaten raw or used in stir-fries.

Sheep Sorrel

Scientific Name: *Rumex acetosella*

Region/habitat the plant is found in:

This plant is commonly found in sunny fields.

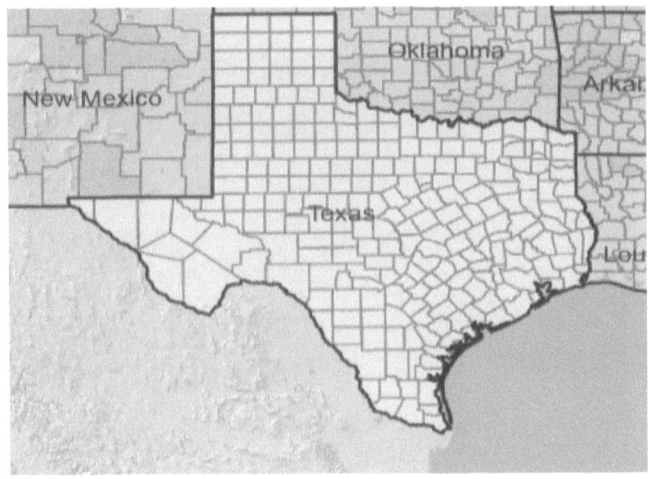

Texas Edible Wild Plant Foraging

Identifying features:

This plant normally achieves a height between 4" and 12" and grows upright. Its stems are reddish and its leaves are arrowhead-shaped and taste sour. They are smooth and are about 1" to 3" long. These leaves grow in a rosette joint at the base of its root system. There are male and female versions of this plant. The male versions produce yellow flowers while the females create green flowers. Fertilized flowers produce seeds that turn red.

Harvesting tips:

The leaves and seeds of this plant can be harvested. Do so as normal.

Seasons for Harvesting: Spring

Preparation/Preservation tips:

- Young leaves can be eaten raw as they have a lemony flavor. Older leaves should be cooked. They can be added to soups.
- Seeds can be toasted.

Spiderwort

Scientific Name: *Tradescantia species*

Region/habitat the plant is found in:

This is a common find in fields and wooded areas across Texas.

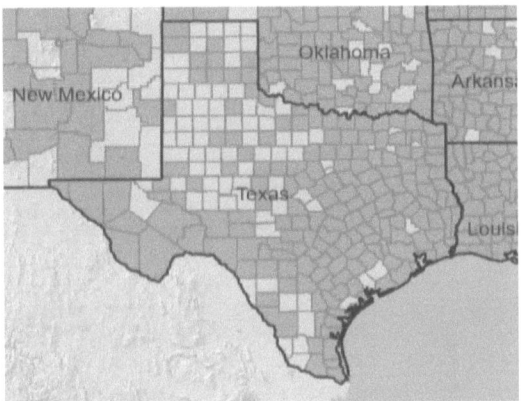

Identifying features:

This plant grows to about 2' tall with an upright stem. It has long leaves with a parallel vein. Its flowers bloom in the morning and tend to close by noon. These 3-petal flowers are normally blue but can turn pink. Spiderworts tend to grow in clusters.

Harvesting tips:

The entire plant is edible but because of the toughness of the stems, my advice is to stick to consuming the leaves, flowers, and flower buds. Harvest as usual.

Seasons for Harvesting: Spring, late summer, fall

Preparation/Preservation tips:

- The plant's stems can be pureed and added to stews as a thickening agent.
- Leaves can be eaten raw and added to salads.
- Flowers and flower buds can be dried and used to make tea.

Texas Edible Wild Plant Foraging

Sweet Potato

Scientific Name: *Ipomoea batatas*

Region/habitat the plant is found in:

This plant is found in landscaped areas.

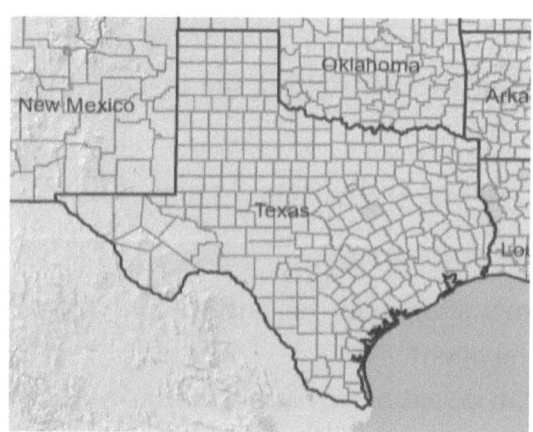

Identifying features:

These plants produce enlarged tubers with purple, red, brown, yellow, or white skin. These tubers tend to take on irregular shapes and sizes. Highly nutritious, they contain minerals, vitamins, protein, and fiber. Above the ground, its leaves are held up by a creeping vine that can achieve a length of about 13'. These leaves are heart-shaped. The plant produces white or purple flowers.

Harvesting tips:

The tubers and leaves of this plant are edible. Dig up the soil around the sweet potatoes to get to the tubers. Harvest the leaves as you normally would.

Seasons for Harvesting: Summer, fall

Preparation/Preservation tips:

- Tubers can be boiled, roasted, and sorted. In fact, these can be used in much the same way that you can use traditional potatoes.
- Leaves can be eaten raw and added to salads.

Texas Dandelion

Scientific Name: *Pyrrhopappus paucifloru*

Region/habitat the plant is found in:

This plant is a common sight along roadsides, disturbed areas, and fields.

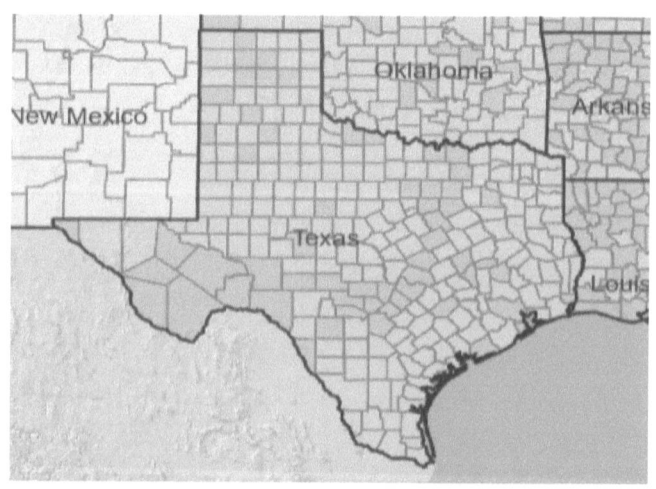

Identifying features:

The Texas dandelion grows to about 20" tall. It has leaves with a sharp spear point. They are green and slender. The long leaves are also deeply notched with a backward-pointing lobe. The plant produces bright yellow flowers that have a purple to black anther in the center. These flowers are typically about 1" across. The flowers tend to bloom in the morning from March to May.

Harvesting tips:

The young leaves, flowers, and roots of this plant are edible. Harvest as usual.

Seasons for Harvesting: Spring

Preparation/Preservation tips:

- Young leaves can be used as bitter greens in salads and can be eaten raw.
- Roots can be dried and ground to create coffee and steeped to make tea.
- Flowers can be steeped to make tea or used to make jellies. Remove the green color of the flower before you do this.

Poisonous Lookalike:

Common Groundsel is a Texas dandelion lookalike. Common Groundsel is an erect plant that grows up to about 1 ½". It also produces yellow flowers like Texas dandelion as well as having narrow leaves. The major difference between the two plants is that while common groundsel flowers do look like dandelions, they never open.

Texas Edible Wild Plant Foraging

Trifoliate Orange

Scientific Name: *Poncirus trifoliat*

Region/habitat the plant is found in:

Found plentifully in partially shaded wooded areas.

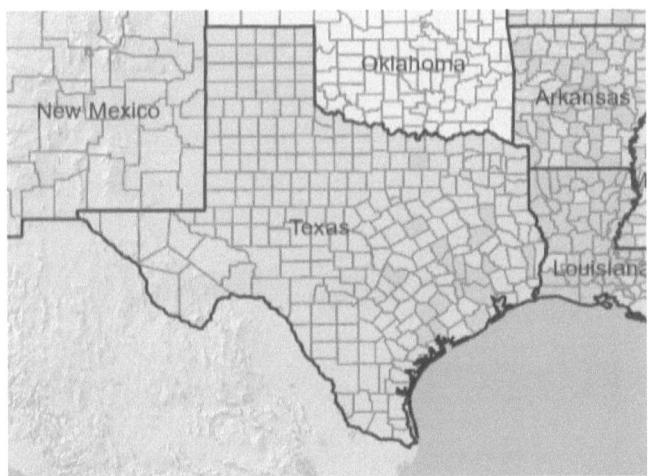

Identifying features:

This plant gets its name from the fact that its leaves (foliate) appear in threes (tri). Also called hardy orange, this plant is a small tree that can grow up to 20' tall. The tree is characterized by bright green twigs that have long spines. These twigs are about 2" long. They are sharps, so beware!

The trifoliate orange produces small lemon-like fruits that are full of seeds and ripen in the fall. These are about the size of golf balls. The fruits are sour like lemons as well. While the fruits are edible, eating too much can cause nausea and an upset stomach.

Harvesting tips:

The mature fruit of these plants is harvestable. Be careful of the spines while gently plucking the fruit off the branches.

Seasons for Harvesting: Late fall

Preparation/Preservation tips:

- The fruit can be juiced. To gain as much juice from this as

Texas Edible Wild Plant Foraging

possible, allow the fruit to sit for about 2 weeks before using a juicer. This makes a refreshing substitute for lemonade especially since it is full of vitamin C.
- The pulp and peel of the fruits can be used to make marmalades.
- The peel can be zested to make cocktails or to use as a seasoning in cooking.

Wine Cup

Scientific Name: *Callirhoe involucrata*

Region/habitat the plant is found in:

These are not a common find in Texas, but when you do find them, typical locations include ditches, abandoned yards, sandy fields, and sunny spaces.

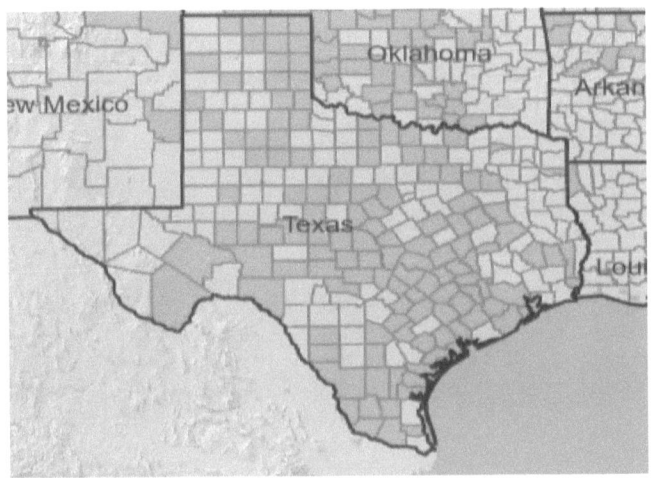

Identifying features:

Also known as poppy mallow, this wildflower is characterized by bright pink flowers resembling wine cups – hence the name. They appear at the top of long stalks and open in the morning while closing in the evening. The flowers have a white spot at the base of the five petals. As beautiful as these flowers are, they are not edible.

This plant grows to about 3' tall and has hairy, round leaves that are deeply lobed.

Harvesting tips:

The tubers and leaves of this plant are edible.

Seasons for Harvesting: All year round

Preparation/Preservation tips:

- The tubers of this plant taste like sweet potatoes and can be eaten raw or cooked.
- The leaves add a thickening quality to soups and stews when cooked.

Texas Edible Wild Plant Foraging

Wireweed

Scientific Name: *Sida rhombifolia, S. acute, S. cordifolia, S. elliottii and S. Espinosa*

Region/habitat the plant is found in:

This is a common sight among shaded and sunny fields, wet areas, disturbed spots and the Texas borders.

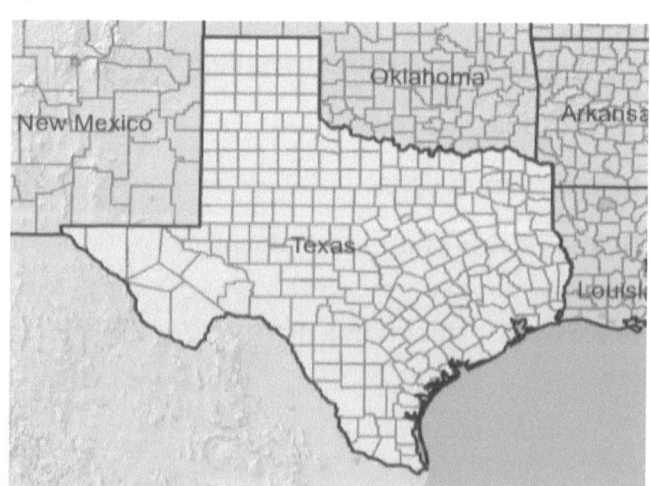

Identifying features:

Wireweed loves to hug the ground and grows to about 3". This plant is characterized by diamond-shaped leaves that are toothed and have a pinnate vein pattern. These leaves are typically ½" long. They are hairy on the undersides and tops and grow in an alternating pattern on branches.

The plant produces yellow flowers with five petals. Small fruits eventually appear in replacement of these flowers. They are green but eventually dry out and turn brown. The stem of this plant can range from green to brown as they dry out. The stems and roots are tough and can be used to make baskets hence the name.

While the plant's roots have medicinal qualities, it contains soap-like qualities and a compound known as ephedrine. Ephedrine can suppress appetite and raise blood pressure as well as lead to a false positive meth drug test.

Harvesting tips:

The leaves of this plant can be harvested. Harvest as usual.

Seasons for Harvesting: Spring, summer, winter

Preparation/Preservation tips:

- Leaves can be steeped to make tea as well as cooked.

Yarrow

Scientific Name: *Achillea millefolium*

Region/habitat the plant is found in:

It is not common to find this plant in many places in Texas but they can be spotted in landscape areas, yards, and sunny fields.

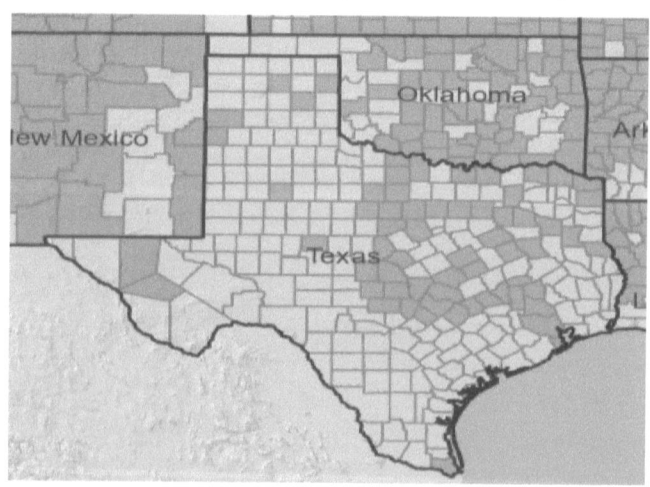

Identifying features:

This plant has no branches and grows up to about 3' tall. Its leaves grow from the stem in an alternating pattern and they are typically between 3" and 5" long. They are compound leaves, and have a fern-like appearance and a leathery texture. The plant produces small white flowers that typically bloom between April and October. Both the leaves and flowers of this plant afront with a spicy scent similar to cooking herbs like rosemary and oregano.

Harvesting tips:

The flowers and leaves of this plant are edible. Harvest as usual.

The main use of the harvestable parts of this plant is medicine but the leaves and flowers can be used to make teas.

Seasons for Harvesting: Summer

Preparation/Preservation tips:

- Flowers and leaves can be steeped to make tea.

Poisonous Lookalike:

Fool's parsley and poison hemlock are poisonous plants that look similar to yarrow. The difference is that yarrow has fuzzy or hairy leaves and stems while these components are smooth on the poisonous lookalikes, which are also characterized by a chemical scent. Consuming the leaves of poison hemlock or fool's parsley leaves can be fatal.

Texas Edible Wild Plant Foraging

Fool's parsley

Poison hemlock

Yucca

Scientific Name: *Yucca spp.*

Region/habitat the plant is found in:

It is common to find this plant in sunny areas across Texas.

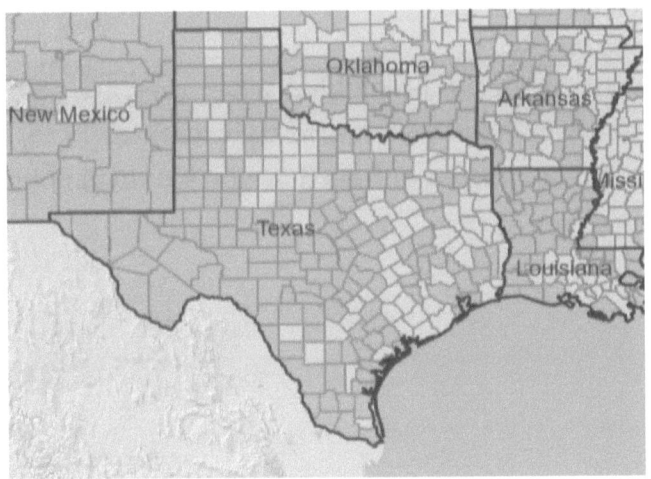

Texas Edible Wild Plant Foraging

Identifying features:

This plant has stiff sword-like leaves and produces white waxy flowers. Its flowers grow in clusters and the leaves originate from the base of the plant. It grows to about 30' tall and is stemless.

Harvesting tips:

The only edible parts of this plant are the fruits, flowers, and flower stalks. Do not consume the rest of this plant as the other parts are poisonous.

It is best to harvest the flowers within the first few days that they open as the taste quickly deteriorates. Taste one of the flowers before you harvest many.

The edible parts can be harvested as normal.

Seasons for Harvesting: Fruit spring to summer, flowers summer to early fall just after they bloom, flower stalks before flowers appear in summer

Preparation/Preservation tips:

- Flowers and flower stalks can be eaten raw or cooked. The flower stalks taste like cauliflower and can be substituted for this vegetable.
- Flowers stalks can be pickled when they are young as they become tough and tasteless as they mature.
- Fruit can be roasted or baked as you would eggplant.

SEASONAL CHART

At a glance, here is when you can harvest the parts of all of the Texan wild plants outlined above:

Plant	Summer	Fall	Winter	Spring
Agave	X	X	X	X
Alligator Weed	X	X		X
Amaranth	X			
Bay Laurel	X	X	X	X
Bastard Cabbage	X	X		X
Beautyberry	X	X		
Cactus - Cow's Tongue	X	X	X	X
Cactus - Prickly Pear	X	X	X	X
Canna Lily	X	X		
Dayflower	X	X		X
Duckweed	X			
Farkleberry		X	X	

Texas Edible Wild Plant Foraging

Frog Fruit	X			X
Ginkgo	X	X		X
Ground Cherry	X	X		
Honey Locust	X			X
Indian Strawberry				X
Japanese Hawkweed		X	X	X
Kudzu	X	X	X	X
Lady's Thumb	X			X
Lizard's Tail	X	X		X
Magnolia	X	X	X	X
Milkweed	X			X
Nasturtium	X			X
Ocotillo	X	X	X	X
Onion – Wild	X	X	X	X

Passion Vine	X	X	X	
Pimpernel	X			X
Pineapple Weed	X	X		X
Queen Anne's Lace	X			
Redbud				X
Sheep Sorrel				X
Spiderwort	X	X		X
Sweet Potato	X	X		
Texas Dandelion				X
Trifoliate Orange		X		
Wine Cup	X	X	X	X
Wireweed	X		X	X
Yarrow	X			
Yucca	X	X		X

POISONOUS PLANTS

Depending on the type of contact with any of the exact plants listed below, consuming or having contact with eyes and skin can cause a variety of detrimental effects. Some of these effects can even be fatal. If you ever come into contact with any of the plants listed or think you have been poisoned by them, immediately contact your local poison center network. Do not wait for symptoms to appear for you to make that call. These symptoms will be listed below each of the poisonous plants stated below. While you wait for help, here are a few treatment options that allow you to minimize the effects:

If a poisonous plant is eaten

First, remove any remaining part of the ingested plant from your mouth and save a piece in a dry container to allow identification by the poison center network. Wash out your mouth with water and check to see if there is any swelling, discoloration, or irritation.

If a poisonous plant comes into contact with the eyes

Wash your hands with soap and water before touching your eyes to avoid further irritation then wash out your eyes with lukewarm tap water for about 10 to 15 minutes.

If a poisonous plant comes into contact with skin

Remove any contaminated clothing that you might have been wearing and wash the affected area well with soap and water.

Carol bean (*Erythrina herbacea*)

Description:

These plants are deceptively beautiful with scarlet red flowers and seeds that are exposed when their peapods, which are almost black, burst open. The colorful display often attracts hummingbirds and insects. These pods are about 8" long. This plant reaches an approximate height of 6' and has compound leaves that grow in an alternate pattern with 3 leaflets that are often prickly on the underside.

Symptoms:

Eating carol bean seeds can lead to hallucinations.

Locoweed (*Genera Astragalus and Oxytropis*)

Description:

This plant does not grow very tall - only between 3' and 5' - and grows in clusters. It produces large, irregular-shaped leaves and flowers that can be purple or white.

Symptoms:

This plant gets its name because it contains a compound that causes cattle to behave erratically when they eat it due to its hallucinogenic properties. It has the same effect on humans and can cause staggering, dehydration, increased heart rate, convulsions, drooling, glazed eyes, and even death depending on the amount consumed.

Mescal Bean (*Dermatophyllum secundiflorum*)

Description:

This is a flowering plant that typically grows to about 10' but can achieve a height of 35' in rare instances. It produces purple flowers that emit a strong smell. From these flowers comes a large fruit that can have between 1 and 8 hard seeds (beans) that come in colors ranging from red to yellow. The compound leaves grow in an alternate pattern with 7 to 13 leaflets.

Symptoms:

Eating seeds of this plant are toxic to humans because of the presence of the compound called quinolizidine alkaloids. Signs of ingestion of this compound include convulsions, hallucinations, severe vomiting, lowered blood pressure, confusion, agitation, increased heart rate, and abdominal pain.

Nightshade (*Solanaceae*)

Description:

This small tree has small pinnate compound leaves that grow in an alternate arrangement. The stems and leaves of this plant are armed with tiny sharp plant hairs. The plant produces flowers that can either be purple, white, or yellow. They bloom in clusters. From these flowers come a berry that looks like an egg. These berries and the leaves of this plant are toxic to humans because of the compound called solanine.

Symptoms:

Ingesting solanine can cause symptoms like diarrhea, vomiting, headaches, nightmares, dizziness, and pain in joints. Death can occur if large amounts are eaten.

Poison Hemlock (*Conium maculatum*)

Description:

This plant can grow up to 10' tall and has distinguishable umbrella-shaped, small white flowers that grow in clusters. Its stem is hollow and has red or purple spots or streaks. Its leaves are fern-like and bright green with toothed edges, and a musty odor is released when they are crushed.

Symptoms:

Eating most parts of this plant leads to a variety of terrible symptoms that include muscle tremors, nervousness, excess salivation, and incoordination. More severe symptoms include partial paralysis, slowed heart rate, lowered body temperature, coma, and even death.

Texas Edible Wild Plant Foraging

Poison Ivy (*Toxicodendron radicans*)

Description:

These are climbing vines that can grow as long as 100'. The characteristic that makes this most identifiable is its 3 leaves, which are similar to that tri-structure of kudzu. These leaves tend to be between 2" and 4" long and are green but may display a reddish tinge. The leaves are smooth and can either be dull or glossy colored. They turn yellow and red in the fall. Leaf edges can either be smooth or lobed.

Symptoms:

This plant causes blisters when it comes into contact with the skin. The compound that causes this blistering is known as urushiol. It binds to the skin quickly and if you wait for longer than 30 minutes to wash this compound off, it can be too late. If this compound comes into contact with clothing, do not burn it as the compound can also be carried in the smoke and get into your nose and throat.

Poison Sumac (*Toxicodendron vernix*)

Description:

A relative to poison ivy, this poisonous plant is typically found in wet areas in East Texas. It also has 3 leaves that emerge from a single stem and is a vine.

Symptoms:

Coming into contact with this plant can cause itchy rashes that blister.

Texas Edible Wild Plant Foraging

Texas Bullnettle (*Cnidoscolus texanus*)

Description:

This plant typically grows between 1 ½' to 4' in height with several stems that emerge from the base. The leaves are typically 2" to 4" long with five lobes and occur in an alternating pattern. They are crinkled in appearance and are covered with stinging needles.

Symptoms:

Coming into contact with the needles of this plant can cause a stinging burn that can lead to an infection known as cellulitis. The affected area becomes red and swollen and is painful and warm to the touch.

Thornapple (*Datura stramonium*)

Description:

This plant can grow to a height of above 3' but is typically found at a much shorter height. Its leaves are dark green and grow in an alternate pattern. They are toothed. The flowers range in color from purple to white and are trumpet-shaped. It has 5 lobes.

Symptoms:

All parts of thornapple are toxic to consume. Consumption leads to symptoms like diarrhea, vomiting, hallucinations, delirium, coma, and even death.

Water Hemlock (*Conium maculatum*)

Description:

This is a plant that typically ranges in height from between 3' and 6'. Its stems can be green, purple, or pink. The compound leaves grow in an alternate pattern and are pinnate-shaped. Water hemlock produces small umbel flowers that grow in clusters.

Symptoms:

All of this plant's parts are poisonous to humans but they are most toxic in the spring. Toxicity is mostly transferred through eating but the toxic compound in the plant but it can be absorbed through touch. Symptoms include nausea, abdominal pain, seizures, vomiting, and even death depending on the amount consumed.

DIRECTORY 2

10 RECIPES FROM WILD PLANTS

The sky's the limit when you think about all the tasty dishes that you can prepare with foraged Texan wild plants, but I have given you 10 go-to recipes that you can always have in your back pocket below.

HONEY LEMON YARROW TEA

Prep time: 5 minutes

Serves: 2

Ingredients:

- 2 tsp. dried yarrow leaves
- 2 tsp. honey
- Lemon slices
- Boiling water

Directions:

1. Dry yarrow leaves in a paper bag for at least 1 week and pulse

to a fine powder in a food processor.
2. Add the yarrow to the boiling water.
3. Sweet with honey.
4. Add lemon slices and serve.

FLORAL QUEEN ANN'S LACE ICED TEA

Prep time: 15 minutes

Serves: 5

Ingredients:

- 20 Queen Ann's Lace flowers
- 2 tsp. lemon juice
- 1 L boiling water
- Sugar to taste

Directions:

1. Add the sugar to the boiling water and stir to dissolve.
2. Stir in the lemon juice and transfer the mixture to a pitcher.
3. Stir in the Queen Ann's Lace flowers and refrigerate the tea for at least 6 hours before serving chilled.

TANGY PASSION FRUIT JUICE

Prep time: 10 minutes

Serves: 5

Ingredients:

- 5 passion fruits

- Juice of 1 lime
- Sugar to taste
- 1 L water

Directions:

1. Slice the passion fruit and extract the pulp and seeds.
2. Add the water. Mix well and strain to remove any further seeds.
3. Stir in the remaining ingredients. Serve chilled or with ice.

SIMPLE SWEET POTATO CHIPS

Prep time: 10 minutes

Serves: 4

Ingredients:

- 1 lb. sweet potatoes, sliced with a mandoline slicer
- Salt and pepper to taste
- ¼ cup olive oil

Directions:

1. Preheat the oven to 300 degrees F.
2. Line a baking sheet with parchment.
3. Toss all the ingredients together in a large bowl and place them in a single layer on the prepared baking sheet.
4. Bake for 20 minutes or until the sweet potatoes are crisp and brown around the edges.
5. Serve warm as is or with desired dip.

ITALIAN DANDELION CHIPS

Prep time: 10 minutes

Serves: 3

Ingredients:

- 3 handfuls Texas dandelion leaves
- ¼ cup olive oil
- 1 tbsp. Italian seasoning

Directions:

1. Preheat the oven to 200 degrees F.
2. Line a baking sheet with parchment.
3. Toss all the ingredients together in a large bowl and place in a single layer on the prepared baking sheet.
4. Bake for 15 minutes or until the leaves are crisp.
5. Serve warm or crush to add texture and flavor to salads and dishes such as mashed potatoes.

SPICY YARROW SCRAMBLED EGGS

Prep time: 5 minutes

Serves: 2

Ingredients:

- 8 eggs
- ⅓ cup grated yarrow
- 1 tbsp. green seasoning blend
- Salt to taste

- ½ tsp cayenne pepper

Directions:

1. Whisk the eggs together with the other ingredients.
2. Heat a non-stick skillet and scrambled eggs to desired softness.
3. Serve warm.

TEXAS DANDELION FRITTERS

Prep time: 15 minutes

Serves: 5

Ingredients:

- 3 cups washed and dried Texas dandelion flowers
- 1 cup all-purpose flour
- Salt and pepper to taste
- 1 large egg, whisked
- 1 cup milk
- Vegetable oil

Directions:

1. Combine all the ingredients except the dandelion flowers and oil to create a fritter batter.
2. Heat the oil in a frying pan over medium heat.
3. Dip each flower into the fritter batter and fry until the edges turn brown then flip to fry until the flower is lightly browned.
4. Drain on paper towels.
5. Drizzle with your favorite toppings such as honey or icing

sugar and serve warm.

PRICKLY PEAR JUICE

Prep time: 10 minutes

Serves: 2

Ingredients:

- 15 prickly pears

Directions:

1. Cut off the ends of the prickly pears.
2. Make a vertical slice along the prickly pears and remove the skin.
3. Extract the juice from the remaining flesh by pulsing it in a food processor. Sieve the mixture and transfer it to a jug.
4. Serve as desired.

GINKGO NUT QUINOA

Prep time: 10 minutes

Serves: 2

Ingredients:

- 30 ginkgo nuts
- 2 cups cooked quinoa
- ½ cup chopped almonds
- 1 tbsp. soy sauce
- ½ cup chopped green onions

- Salt and pepper to taste

Directions:

1. Remove ginkgo nuts from the shells and dip them in boiling water to peel off the outer skin easily.
2. Combine all the ingredients in a bowl.
3. Serve with your favorite condiment.

WILD ONION CREAMY SOUP

Prep time: 10 minutes

Serves: 4

Ingredients:

- 3 bunches of wild onion, rinsed and roots trimmed.
- 1 cup heavy cream
- 3 garlic cloves, minced
- 3 tbsp. butter
- Salt and pepper to taste

Directions:

1. Heat the butter in a skillet over medium heat and saute the wild onions for 5 minutes.
2. Stir in garlic and cook for about 2 minutes or until the garlic becomes fragrant.
3. Add the cream and mix. Cook for about 2 minutes so that the liquid reduces slightly.
4. Season with salt and pepper and serve warm.

Leave a 1 click review!

Customer Reviews

★★★★★ 2
5.0 out of 5 stars

5 star		100%
4 star		0%
3 star		0%
2 star		0%
1 star		0%

See all verified purchase reviews

Share your thoughts with other customers

Write a customer review

SINCE SELF-PUBLISHERS REALLY DEPEND ON READERS' REVIEWS, I WOULD BE INCREDIBLY GRATEFUL IF YOU COULD TAKE 60 SECONDS TO WRITE A BRIEF REVIEW ON AMAZON, EVEN IF JUST A FEW SENTENCES.
PLEASE SCAN ON THE QR CODE BELOW TO LEAVE A REVIEW.
THANK YOU!

CONCLUSION

Foraging is the activity that allowed our ancestors to survive. They took what the land gave and, apart from the threat of dangers like wild animals and disease, they thrived physically where they had access to wild plants. These plants benefited them in many ways. They gave them resources for medication and shelter and were used as tools, some of the biggest advantages apart from food. These benefits are still available to us modern-day human beings. Foraging can supply you with all your nutritional needs, virtually eliminating your grocery bill. Foraging can provide you with 100% natural and organic food while bringing you closer to nature for a greater appreciation of all the abundance it provides.

We can only sustainably gain these benefits if we ethically go about reaping the seeds that nature sows. The principles of ethical and sustainable foraging include:

1) Forage mindfully, with a mindset to take only what you need.
2) Take care of nature so that it continues to take of you by participating in practices like spreading seeds after you have harvested a plant.
3) Pursue continuous learning to understand the plants you harvest and the environments in which they grow.

Texas Edible Wild Plant Foraging

Applying these principles ensures you understand:

- The short-term and long-term consequences of foraging on the environment, humans, and the plants themselves.
- How accurate plant identification is possible.
- How to forage safely to avoid poisoning or harming yourself during harvesting trips.

This book was written with specifications for the rules of foraging in the beautiful state of Texas and the particular plants that can be found there. Texas is wild, beautiful, and full of nutritious edible wild plants. And it is high time that you grab your gear and set out to find what the natural habitats of Texas hold in store for you. Remember to forage responsibly and ethically, and always ask for permission when accessing private land. Only eat wild plants when you have 100% identified them.

When in doubt, it is always safe to ask. In fact, going on hikes with an expert is one surefire way to learn plant identities. Use technology to your advantage to access Texas-specific websites and apps that allow doing this. You can always use your smartphone to log the location of where you found an unidentifiable plant, along with a picture of its defining features.

The aim of creating this book was to arm you with as much information as possible before you venture into the Texan wild. You have gotten to the end of this resource. Now, go out there and explore nature's bounty... the wilds of Texas await.

Foraging is my passion, and I hope that it becomes a passion for you, too. This book is not just meant to bring people closer to nature, but also to spread awareness of all the nutritious plants that nature holds in its lap for us. This guide is also an attempt to help people realize how their actions directly contribute to nature's conservation, and how through ethical and responsible foraging, they can make it all the more worthwhile.

Willow Walsh

I'd love to know what you have found out on your trips exploring the wide selection of edible plants in the state of Texas, and what you have made out of it. Head over to Amazon.com and share your experience with this guide, and in exploring the Texan wildlands.

Texas Edible Wild Plant Foraging

A FREE GIFT TO OUR READERS

20 EDIBLE WILD PLANT RECIPES

www.willowwalsh.com

Willow Walsh

FREE GIFT TO OUR READER

FORAGING JOURNAL PDF DOWNLOAD

Willow Walsh

REFERENCES

(PDF) Urban foraging: Its role in conservation and green space management in London. (2019, August 28). ResearchGate. https://www.researchgate.net/publication/337497053_Urban_Foraging_Its_Role_in_Conservation_and_Green_Space_Management_in_London

10 guidelines for ethical foraging. (2018, February 15). https://www.finedininglovers.com/article/10-guidelines-ethical-foraging

(n.d.). AustinTexas.gov. https://www.austintexas.gov/sites/default/files/files/Watershed/invasive/2013_Invasives_guide_small.pdf

The benefits of wild edibles – Mother Earth news. (2014, April 21). Mother Earth News – The Original Guide To Living Wisely. https://www.motherearthnews.com/natural-health/nutrition/benefits-wild-edibles-zeoz1404zjhar/

Brandywine conservancy. (n.d.). Brandywine Conservancy and Museum of Art. https://www.brandywine.org/conservancy/blog/invasive-species-spotlight-foraging-invasives

Communications, & Smith, S. (n.d.). Texas Parks & Wildlife Department. https://tpwd.texas.gov/

Foraging (article) | 6. Early humans | Khan Academy. (n.d.). Khan Academy. https://www.khanacademy.org/humanities/big-history-project/early-humans/how-did-first-humans-live/a/foraging

Foraging laws. (n.d.). Forage Culture. https://www.forageculture.com/foraging-laws

Morelle, R. (2016, May 9). *Kew report makes new tally for number of world's plants.* BBC News. https://www.bbc.com/news/science-environment-36230858

Plants, the 'core basis for life on earth', under increasing threat, warns UN food agency. (2019, December 5). UN News. https://news.un.org/en/story/2019/12/1052591

Texas plant life. (n.d.). TX Almanac. https://www.texasalmanac.com/articles/texas-plant-life

Want to forage in your city? There's a map for that. (2013, April 23). NPR.org. https://www.npr.org/sections/thesalt/2013/04/23/178603623/want-to-forage-in-your-city-theres-a-map-for-that

Why foraging — Arthur Haines. (n.d.). Arthur Haines. https://www.arthurhaines.com/why-foraging

Questions or Concerns?

Please email me at hello@willowwalsh.com

www.ingramcontent.com/pod-product-compliance
Ingram Content Group UK Ltd.
Pitfield, Milton Keynes, MK11 3LW, UK
UKHW041305180426
11947UKWH00009B/698